MW01166739

Back Yard Ovens

EARTH GARDEN BOOKS
Trentham, Victoria

Published by
EARTH GARDEN BOOKS
PO Box 2
Trentham,
Victoria, 3458,
AUSTRALIA.
Phone (03) 5424 1819 Fax (03) 5424 1743.
Email: info@earthgarden.com.au.
Website: www.earthgarden.com.au
A.C.N. 086 043 567
A.B.N. 69 086 043 567

© Copyright Earth Garden Pty Ltd 2007
   Reprinted 2008

ISBN 978-0-9578947-1-6

All rights reserved. No part of this publication may be reproduced, stored in a retrieval system, or transmitted in any form or by any means, electronic, mechanical, photocopying, recording, or otherwise, without the ex-press permission of the publishers, except in the case of brief quotation embodied in critical articles and review.

This book is printed on plantation-grown paper in the interests of preserving our planet's precious resources.

Editor: Alan Gray
Editorial Co-ordinator: Fiona Tunnicliff
Sub-editor: Peter Parsons
Graphic design: Tony Fuery

Distributed by NDD, Melbourne, and Brumby Books, Kilsyth, Melbourne.

DISCLAIMER
Due to the variability of local conditions, materials, skills, site and other such factors, Earth Garden Pty Ltd assumes no liability for personal injury, property damage, or loss of any kind whatsoever arising from actions inspired by information in this book.
The publishers and author cannot accept responsibility for any errors or omissions, or for any claim arising from the use of the book or any information contained in it.
The information contained in this book is of a general nature, and is not intended to be a substitute for professional advice.

Front Cover: John Reid and Thaïs Sansom, from Red Beard Bakery at Trentham in Central Victoria, in front of their newly-built Alan Scott-style brick oven.

Inset: Harry Gray removes some perfectly-cooked naan bread from his family's homemade cob oven, while a prawn pizza (above him) from the same oven is nearly ready.

Back Cover: Kate Schuler inspects the groovy tile inlays in a Terracotta Tile Company DIY pizza oven. See page 77.

Contents

Introduction

I HOPE you enjoy reading this book as much as we enjoyed putting it together. Making your own pizza dough, 'building' your own culinary masterpiece, and then cooking it to perfection on the hot floor of your own wood-fired oven is truly a delightfully sensuous experience!

We hope you'll enjoy reading about how other people have built their own, and we hope this inspires you to have a go at building your oven — it's not hard!

But it is satisfying, and will lead you to a new back yard lifestyle that's quite different to a barbecue lifestyle. Of course why not build your oven next to the barbecue? I can tell you which one will get more use within a month or two!

All the ovens here have been built by real life people, with real life budget and time constraints — forget the instant makeover by polished professionals in super-tight singlets. This book is about getting down and dirty, so that YOU are the one who gets the satisfaction from doing it yourself.

When you come to fire your oven, please think about the source of your firewood. Please don't use firewood that comes from our diminishing native forests — our native animals and plants and rivers — and frogs and birds — need it more than we do.

The good news is that there are vast quantities of plantation timber offcuts available in many States; and even easier to find are mountains of free secondhand wood going to waste in every town in Australia. If you live anywhere near a new housing estate, go hunting through the skip bins outside the half-built houses: you'll come home with a huge pile of kiln-dried wood all ready to be chopped into lengths on a $90 cut-off saw.

Use this sort of wood, and you save it from going to landfill tips where it will simply end up releasing Greenhouse gases as it rots under the ground. Then you get the double satisfaction of knowing that this back yard project is good for your taste buds, and good for the planet.

Enjoy!

Alan T Gray
Publisher.

Chapter One

Cob, Clay
& Earth

Doug's Earth Oven

Inspired by Middle Eastern earth ovens, Doug overcame all manner of obstacles and built his own. Here he describes the process and sums up the results.

by Doug Falconer
CASTLEMAINE, VICTORIA

EVER since visiting Cyprus and Greece 12 years ago, I've had a hankering for a backyard earth oven, just like it seems everyone has over there. It stayed a pipedream until recently, when I got my hands on a neat little book from our Good Life Book Club. Forget *The Da Vinci Code* — *Build Your Own Earth Oven* became my newest unputdownable bestseller — I hungrily read it through to familiarise myself with the process. Not much later, we started some building and paving work in the backyard and it occurred to me that, amongst the mess, all the ingredients were right there around me. The last excuse for delay evaporated.

I asked our long-suffering stonemason to leave an oven-sized opening with a flat floor in the curved wall he was making, and went inside to read the book again. I should have read it more carefully, because when I put on the work clothes the next weekend to begin, I realised I didn't have the 21 house bricks I needed, or at least the right ones. I had missed the bit about them needing to be newish fired bricks with a flat face. All my carefully stacked clean bricks were a bit old and soft, and had frogs on both sides — no good for my purpose. I rang a few friends but no-one could help me

out, so I hopped in the car and drove the 30 minutes to Bendigo to arrive at the brickworks two minutes too late. All those perfect bricks two metres away — behind a barbed wire fence! And to make matters worse, someone had forgotten to lock the front door, so when I knocked and went in, the burglar alarm went off. Boy, my day was getting better and better.

After that, I actually stooped to driving around an estate where a few McMansions were being built, hoping to liberate some spare bricks — with no luck. On the way home, having resigned myself to another delay, I stopped at our landscaping supplies place to pay the account. And the first thing I saw after getting out of the car? A pallet of Bendigo brickworks house bricks for 40 cents each. They couldn't believe I only wanted 21, and I couldn't believe I'd just driven 80 kilometres and wasted half the day to find them just near home.

I quickly made the base from a layer of sand and then the bricks, 'kissing' them into place as the book suggested. It took a couple of goes to get it right, but soon I was ready to make the sand form — 'forming the void'. Following instructions carefully now, I drew the circle and piled the moist builder's sand into the shape that was to become the interior space of the finished oven. It was fun! Sandcastles with a purpose.

Forming the void on the base: 21 bricks on a layer of sand.

Add the 75 mm thermal layer.

Cover the void with wet newspaper.

When it was right, I smoothed it with a piece of wood and covered it with wet newspaper to make it easier to tell where the sand stopped when the time came to remove the sand.

Last thing for the day, I made some test balls of earth to figure out how much sand I needed to add to the mix. While excavating for the paving, we had created several piles of different soils, so I could mix and match. I did the drop test on all the balls, and decided on a mix of about two thirds subsoil and one third sand.

Luckily for me, the next day I had some help from my mate Jeremy, because the mixing involves quite a bit of heaving of mix on a tarp. More messy fun followed as we did the Twist on the mud mix to mix the sand and clay thoroughly, pausing to heave it back and forth on the tarp until it was evenly mixed. Then we dragged it over to the work area and began to make the first 'thermal' layer, which forms the innermost surface of the oven. This involves working small balls of mix in your hands and then pushing them together around the form to make a layer about 75mm thick. It went slowly to begin with, but sped up as we got the hang of it and as we got further up the sloping walls of the sand form.

After a couple of hours of bending over working, we were quite pleased to put the final bit of cob into the top of the oven. Then we got to whack the whole thing with bits of four-by-two to bind it all together. It was late on Sunday evening and I wasn't convinced the structure was strong enough yet, so decided to wait a week for it to dry a little before cutting the door hole. By the next weekend it was firm but still moist and I cut the hole easily with an old kitchen knife. Some bright spark has figured out that the height of the door should be 63 per cent of the interior height of the oven to allow the fire to burn best, so I carefully measured it. I also remembered to make it wide enough for a pizza tray. Then I got down and pulled all the sand

The insulating layer is 120-mm cob.

out, feeling for the newspaper I'd covered the form with. Then it was time to mix more cob, this time with straw added to make an insulating layer, thicker than the thermal layer — about 120 mm thick.

Despite being thicker, this went quicker, and pretty soon we'd finished the second layer. All it needed now was a render to help keep out the elements and make it look a little tidier. I'd always wanted to make a cow manure render, so we headed out to a local farm,

Rendering with cow manure, clay and sand.

Clean the floor with the moistened scuffle.

Hot to trot.

After three hours, rake out the coals.

gathered some fresh manure, and made a quick, wettish mix of manure, sieved clay and a little sand. It wasn't at all unpleasant, though it was difficult to convince Lilly of that. Then we smeared it on the oven and stood back to admire our handiwork. Whoops, no door!

So I joined two pieces of redgum slab I had lying around, shaped it roughly to the hole with a saw, then planed/rasped/sanded it and cut away a little more from around the door hole until it fitted snugly. Once the door was on, the whole effect was like our own little hobbit house in the backyard. All we needed

to do now was … wait. Wait for it to dry, and for the perfect time to inaugurate it.

A couple of weeks later, it seemed dry enough to try out, so I lit a little fire and built it up gradually. It seemed to go well, no sign of choking that some people report. Then I remembered I hadn't made the tools I needed — a 'rake' to scoop out the coals, a 'scuffle' to clean out the floor after removing the fire, and a 'peel' to put the pizzas in and take them out. So while the fire did its thing, I grabbed an old hoe and cut the handle down for a rake, used the bit of handle with a

In with the pizzas.

After five minutes take them out of the trays and lie them on the floor of the oven.

The verdict? Nothing beats homemade wood-fired earth oven pizza.

strong eyelet in the end and tied five two-foot lengths of old towel on it with some wire for a scuffle, and cut a peel out of a fence paling, bevelling the end with the trusty planer. Easy!

Damn, forgot to make the pizzas! Quick — yeast into warm milk/water/sugar for ten minutes, add to flour and warm water, knead for five minutes, place in a warm place to rise for half an hour. Chop the mushrooms, capsicum, Danish fetta, garlic, olives, mozzarella. Knock down the dough, knead it again, roll it out onto the trays, add the tomato paste, toppings, fresh herbs, cheese and olive oil. Phew!

After the fire had been going three hours (the last 30 minutes without fresh fuel so the coals burn down), it's a snap to use the rake to pull out the coals into a tin bucket (or a brazier to keep you warm), then use the moistened scuffle to clean the floor of the oven

— watch the steam rising and feel the heat. It's best to then put the door on and leave it alone for 15 to 20 minutes to 'soak' — so the heat gets evenly distributed. Then it's in with the pizzas! Literally five minutes later, they are done — get them out of the trays for a quick go straight on the bricks (just like a real pizza parlour), then we finally get to eat.

And the verdict? Fantastic! There's nothing like homemade, wood-fired, earth oven pizza. And as the oven cools, you can bake bread, roast vegies (or meat if you're that way inclined), make pies, biscuits or puddings, anything you do in a regular oven. When the baking's over, throw in the wood you'll use to get the next firing going to dry thoroughly. Nothing is wasted!

And when the oven is not being used, which I'll admit is most of the time, it's a fair conversation starter — and everyone wants one in their own backyard.

Making a Mudbrick Beehive Oven

Rob Bakes — gourmet pizza cook and ringmaster of the Mud Brick Circus in Victoria — believes that an oven should be a priority on your building list, once you have bought your land. "What, before the house?" you say. Yes, says Rob, because when you start cooking and serving delicious pizza from your wood-fired oven, not only will you never want to eat a standard pizza again, but you'll have hordes of willing helpers at your gate to assist you with your house building.

by Rob Bakes
KYNETON, VICTORIA

ONCE you've purchased your land, my advice is to make the building of an oven a priority. Learn to cook a good pizza in it and you will have queues of willing helpers at the gate ready to help you build your house. If you crave seclusion, treat the existence of your oven with secrecy. Such an oven is synonymous with sociability and good company. It has the potential to pick up those tenuous threads of human interaction lost in a push-button society that demands instant gratification.

The oven described here is large enough for a number of people to meet for a communal bread-bake.

Materials
• Approximately 200 puddled mudbricks (250 by 375 by 130 mm) plus one to two cubic metres of soil for mortar and the base for the oven tiles.
• Cement plus materials for concrete or cement-stabilised earth.
• Reinforcing — wire netting or scrap steel will do, or use trench mesh.
• Wheel and tyre (13-inch) for an arch support or construct one out of timber. For a rectangular-shaped opening, use a wooden lintel.
• Dome gauge — may be constructed out of timber or metal (Figure 1).
• Solid, wire-cut bricks or terracotta tiles.
• Door, door frame, and door lintel (Figure 2).
• Bolt.
• Weather seal, or linseed oil and mineral turps.

Fabrication
The dome gauge, door, door frame, and lintel can be made fairly easily (by yourself or a tradesperson). The diagrams of each piece include the dimensions you'll need to follow. The door components need to be metal, but the dome gauge can be timber or metal.

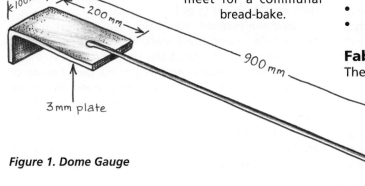

Figure 1. Dome Gauge

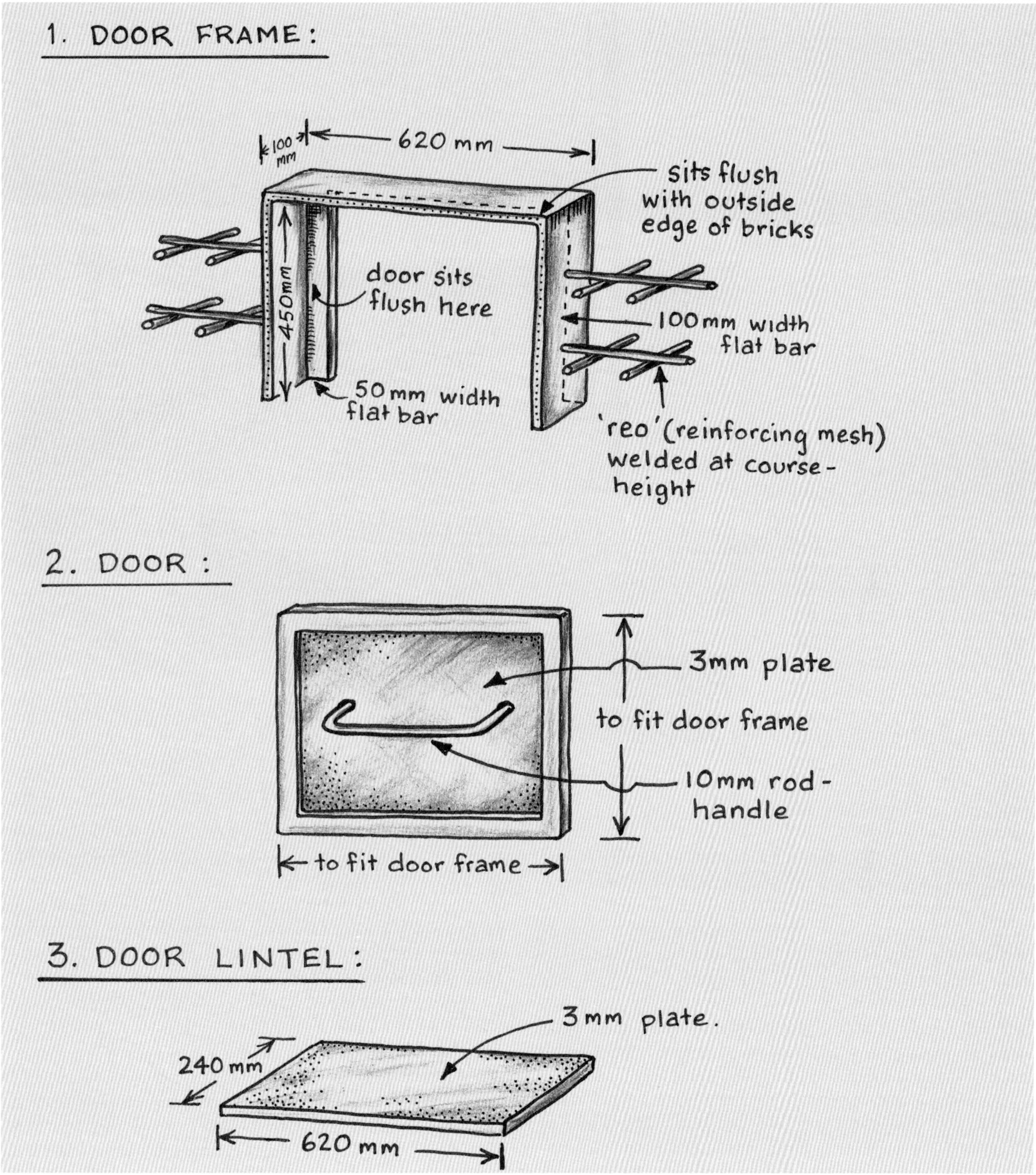

1. DOOR FRAME:

620 mm
100 mm
450 mm
100 mm

Sits flush with outside edge of bricks

door sits flush here

50 mm width flat bar

100mm width flat bar

'reo' (reinforcing mesh) welded at course-height

2. DOOR:

3mm plate

to fit door frame

10mm rod-handle

to fit door frame

3. DOOR LINTEL:

3mm plate.

240 mm

620 mm

Figure 2. Door, door frame, and door lintel

Footings

Drive a 1100 mm stake or piece of steel in the ground, making sure it is plumb. (It needs to be this high because you will use it as a guide for positioning the bricks of the lower part of the structure — to make it even easier mark each course height at 145 mm on the stake.)

Attach a cord to the stake and mark out two circles, one of 820 mm radius to sit inside one of 1220 mm radius (Figure 3). Dig a trench 200 mm deep between the two circles for footings. Pour concrete or stabilised earth in the bottom of the trench and lay in some scrap steel or reinforcing mesh or bar towards the base of the trench. Then fill the trench to ground level. Using mudbricks for formwork, bring the footing up to 125 mm above ground level.

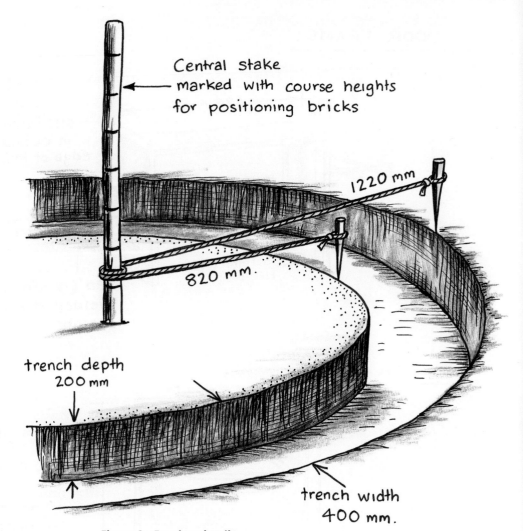

Central stake marked with course heights for positioning bricks

1220 mm

820 mm.

trench depth
200 mm

trench width
400 mm.

Figure 3. Footing detail.

Once the footing has hardened, roll out some dampcourse on the footing and begin laying mudbricks. Adjust the length of your cord to 900 mm and use it to position the bricks in a circle on the footings. Use a level to check the bricks are at the same height all around. Standard mudbricks are 250 by 130 by 375 mm and your course height should be comfortable at 145 mm.

If you want to include an arched doorway in the lower section, use the 13-inch tyre and wheel for your formwork. As you take the brickwork up, tie the arch into the walls with barbed wire or some form of reinforcing. Place the bricks for the arch longways (375 mm) to allow for the curve in the wall.

A small doorway, say three courses high and 400 mm wide, with a lintel, will do just as well as an arch. Build at least one glass flagon into the back of this section, opposite the doorway, to let light in.

Continue the brickwork to one course below waist height. At this stage you need to put in the floor of the oven, so that the baker/cook/operator/cleaner doesn't have to scrabble around at ground level to use the oven.

Slab

You'll need a platform to support this slab floor. A sheet of old corrugated iron with props to support it under the weight of the wet concrete does the job. Cut some face bricks and lay them around the edge. Pour about 50 mm of concrete or stabilised earth over the whole area. Lay some wire netting or reinforcing on this before pouring the rest of the concrete level with the top of the face bricks.

Bury a bolt in the centre of the slab with the head protruding about ten mm — this will be the centre reference for the dome gauge. Leave the slab for at least four days to go off and leave the props in place.

Now the fun really begins — the dome.

Using the dome gauge

Once you're happy that the slab is stable enough for you to stand on (still with the props in place), rest the tail of the gauge against the bolt in the centre of the slab. Sit the brick inside the angle at the other end, lower it into position on the mortar. The gauge ensures that all the bricks follow a uniform tilt (Figure 4). The bolt in the slab should allow you to pivot the angled tail of the gauge quite easily to get it into position to guide the next brick into place. Continue around, and do each course in the same way.

Locating the door

Place the door frame on the slab. Use the dome gauge to position the top, outside corners of the door frame flush with the outside of the oven. Place

Dome Gauge

prop

slab

props

Figure 4. The dome gauge ensures that all the bricks follow a uniform tilt.

I find that it's easier to finish off with a spiral pattern to close the dome than try to follow the concentric circles used so far. If your bricks are dry you can remove the formwork soon after you have finished the last of the brickwork. Crawl inside the oven and point up and wash down the inside immediately. Then do the same outside. With mudbricks it is essential to complete pointing up and washing down while the brickwork is still green.

Pave the slab with bricks or tiles. Lay the bricks in a bed of mud but with no mortar between them. Protect the oven from the weather until you are satisfied that everything is dry, then render the oven and treat it with a waterproofing material.

the door lintel over the frame, using mud under the outside edge to achieve the required tilt.

Laying dome bricks
The mortar course must be thick on the outside edge but thinner on the inside to help get the necessary tilt. Increase the course height for dome bricks to 160 mm. Check for level as you lay each brick.

As the dome builds, each circle becomes smaller so you'll need to adjust the size of bricks and the width of the vertical joins as necessary to maintain the bond through the courses. The tendency of the bricks to fall off the wall increases as the dome progresses, so you will need to support them with sticks or stakes for a while after you lay them. I find that I only need enough props for one course. By the time I start a new layer, the first prop from the proceeding layer can be removed.

Once the dome is to the stage where there is only just room to stand in the hole, crawl out through the door. Bend some strips of steel sheet to fill in the hole and prop them so the dome shape is maintained. You'll need to erect a scaffold so you can lay the last stage of the dome from the top of the oven.

Cooking in your oven
Light the fire in the middle of the oven towards the back. Once the fire is established, pile it up with wood — the flames may lick out through the top of the door while the air is sucked in the bottom. After about an hour of intense heat the roof of your oven will lose its blackness and go light in colour.

For cooking pizzas, rake the coals to one side. Clean the floor with a wet mop and cook directly on the bricks. Occasionally add wood to keep the oven temperature constant. Leave the door off.

To bake bread, you can rake all the coals out of the oven and mop the whole area. After placing the risen dough on the oven floor, close the door while the loaves bake.

Illustrations redrafted — after Bronwyn Halls in 'The Earth Builder's Handbook', [Greg Simmons and Alan T. Gray (Eds), Earth Garden Books, 1996] — by Kathie Hollis 2006.

Basic cob oven on rock and concrete base with timber and mini-orb roof.

Cob Oven: Clare As Mud

Clare built her oven over a weekend with a little help from the kids. She didn't really know what she was doing, she says, but the proof of her success is in the eating.

by Clare Staines
CROWS NEST, QUEENSLAND

I didn't really have any idea what I was doing when I built my cob oven, but was working under the wisdom that it is better to start and learn on the way than plan forever and never get around to doing anything. I started with a 1.25 m square by 400 mm high rock base set into the ground about 100 mm, with the intention of building a brick oven. Old shelving, the height I wanted, held up with stakes made a reasonable formwork. Layered rocks flat-side(ish) faced the formwork and were backfilled with concrete and smaller rocks. The top of the base was fairly rough and ready, but level.

Shortly after the rock base was finished, our local Community Organic Gardens advertised a cob oven building workshop. Twenty people had a dirty day dancing in mud, building an oven and getting elbow deep in fresh cowpats. My change in direction from brick to cob began from there.

The instruction sheet from the workshop gave exact details on how to build a basic cob oven, so I followed their dimensions to make a small oven with no chimney with internal dimensions of 700 mm diameter and 400 mm height. The walls are 150 mm thick and the door opening 250 mm (about 60 per cent of the oven height) with a lip of about 40 mm to stop the door from falling in.

'Door catches fire' episodes
Firebricks were laid on a layer of sand on top of the base, kept in place with rocks mortared into place surrounded with free-form mosaic. The oven itself was built using local barley straw and local red clay soil, rendered with a mix of fresh horse manure, red clay, lime and sump oil. The whole lot is protected with a 1.5 m square mini-orb roof which makes a handy spot to rest the pizza paddle and torch. The door was temporary, made from some scraps of tongue-and-groove, with tin nailed to the oven-side after a couple of 'door catches fire' episodes before I worked out that you don't use the door when the fire's burning. It works fine, so a proper door has

To save money, the fire bricks were placed only in the oven area. They are held in place with rocks and free-form mosaic.

never been made.

I built the oven over a weekend with occasional help from the kids — mostly because I still didn't really know what I was doing. It's kind of stressful when people are standing around expecting you to bark instructions, and instead you mutter vague phrases about seeing how it goes.

While there was lots of information about building an oven, there isn't much about cooking in one. Even simple stuff like preparing the oven and getting pizzas on and off the paddle weren't straightforward (I suspect calzone were invented from pizzas that wouldn't slip onto the paddle properly) and we took a while to work it all out. Every burnt loaf or ashy pizza has added to our body of knowledge and very little ends up being completely inedible (and nothing is inedible if you have dogs or chickens).

The first trick is a good fire started a couple of hours before you want to cook. We use lots of smallish timber up to wrist thickness to start off, but if we are busy and don't want to keep checking the oven, we use bigger pieces, as long as they are dry, fast-burning timber. The fallen dead timber from our eucalypts in the extended bush garden is ideal.

Then, when it's a red-hot heap, most of the embers are scooped out with a shovel and placed in a metal bucket. The rest of the embers are pushed to the back and sides of the oven – it seems to work better with a bit of residual heat happening. The firebricks are cleaned off with a damp rag tied to the end of a stick and the door closed for a while to even the heat out.

A tip for preparing pizza if you don't want floury bases — get the dough ready and let the tops dry just enough so they aren't sticky. Then flip them over, add the toppings and the paddle slips under easily.

RECIPE

Naan breads

I make big batches and freeze them to accompany curries and dips. The dough can be prepared in a bread maker if you've got one.

Mix 150 ml of warm milk, 1 teaspoon of sugar and 2 teaspoons of dried yeast and let stand for 10 minutes to froth up.

Sift 450 g bread flour, 1/2 teaspoon of salt and 1 teaspoon of baking powder together and place in a large bowl. Add the yeast mixture, another teaspoon of sugar, 2 tablespoons of vegetable oil, 150 ml of plain yoghurt and one egg. Mix well, then knead for 10 minutes.

Set aside in a warm place (the car is a good spot — use the windows to control the temperature) until the dough has doubled in size.

Knead again and divide into 6 balls for large breads or 12 for smaller ones. Roll the balls out into oval/tear shaped shapes between 5 and 10 mm thick. Cook directly on the floor of the prepared oven – work fast as they cook quickly and are ready when they are puffed up and golden brown. For variations, add a tablespoon of whole cumin, poppy, onion or sesame seeds to the dough mix.

Willie the Wombat Bread Oven

Willie the Wombat snoozes between firings.

by Chris and Louise Gibson
AINSLIE, ACT

OUR bread oven was built step-by-step with Kiko Denzer's book in one hand and great lumps of mud in the other. The bricks for the base came out of a Sydney garden and the base cunningly incorporates a wood store. This is ideal snake habitat and can be slightly alarming when it is time to rake out the coals. We didn't do any soil tests but the cracks haven't got too big yet and Willie's nose is still attached.

Quite soon I will finish the chimney and intend to make a square door frame out of angle iron to make fitting the firing door easier. At the moment the entrance is getting knocked about a bit and the door keeps catching fire.

Our first attempts at bread making were fairly dismal as we kept running out of day before the oven was hot enough. The inside really does glow red when optimum heat is reached. Pizzas, very simple to make, have alone made the whole exercise worthwhile and once our house is built we might build a masonry bread oven as well. In the mean time Willie the Wombat oven is doing a sterling job.

Pizzas – very simple to make – have alone made the whole exercise worthwhile.

Wood-fired ovens can be almost any shape or size. In this case, Jill decided she wanted to keep hers small and simple.

by Jill Redwood

GOONGERAH, VICTORIA

AFTER scouring the internet to find out how to build a cob oven I discovered that there's no right or wrong way — just many different versions of getting a big dome built that will retain and radiate heat.

They can be big, small, long and arched, deep and domed, brick, clay, mud, with or without fibre, with or without chimney and even with or without adornments.

I ended up deciding on a small one-person cob oven, enough for one pizza tray or two trays of baked vegies at a time. To build it up to comfortable working height I used old bricks to make two walls, a few pieces of hefty timber for the bearers on top of the walls, a sheet of corrugated iron on top of them with cement slapped in the grooves, then old firebricks laid on top and fixed with more cement between the bricks. That gave a good heat-retaining bottom for the oven to sit on. It also made a handy space to keep wood underneath.

A good barrow load of wet sand was brought up from the river and a dome was made on top of the bricks to be the size of the space I wanted inside

Using grey clay with sand naturally mixed through, Jill built up the layers of cob with a few broken sticks to help hold the adjoining clay balls in place.

the oven. I covered this in plastic (recycled from when the newsagents would plastic wrap my weekly paper. Humph.).

The door was from an old wood stove and I made the height of the oven's top about twice the height of the door space. I decided not to have a chimney as it seemed better to have the heat from the fire curl around inside and back out the door. No chimney hole means the heat is kept inside while baking too.

The neighbour upriver had excavated a shed site on a silt delta. This was grey clay with a good measure of sand naturally mixed through. Two barrow loads of that was plenty.

I started off by making the clay sticky and workable. Not too wet, not too dry. When I had 20 or so fist-sized balls of clay I started building up the first layer. Each round of mud balls I'd poke finger holes in for keying in the next layer with a few broken sticks to help hold the adjoining clay balls in place. This wasn't anything I'd read, it just seemed a good thing to do.

I put the door in place for the first round and built the cobs around it.

The oven ended up with three layers of cob to give it plenty of heat-holding thermal mass. It could have done with more but I ran out of room on the brick base. When it had dried out after a week or so of good summer heat, I took out the sand castle inside that had been the mould, and set a small fire going inside to slowly dry it out. The drying out made many small cracks as you'd expect, so I plastered more clay into those.

The final coat was a you-beaut deep red clay from another local source a few farms down the road, just 'coz it looks warm and rich. I used a tad of cement in that to help it weather better. Then for the finishing folly — I sculpted a kookaburra and cockatoo to lean against the oven sides warming their bottoms, and on top, a quoll to curl up in the warmth as they do to sun themselves on rocky warm high spots.

You need good wood to get a cob oven hot — just like with a wood stove. So as well as using up all the odd bits of woody shrapnel, throw in some decent lumps of wood as well for a good hour or more. Mine's ready when the dome is too hot to hold a hand on for long. Let it burn down, scrape out the coals or push them to the back, throw in the food (either straight onto the hot base or on a grate), put the door in the hole, sit back, listen to the crickets, watch the wild ducks wing home for the evening and smell that tucker cooking ... earth, air, fire and food — bliss.

For the finishing folly Jill sculpted a quoll curled up on top in the warmth.

RECIPES

Tasty Baked Pumpkin

Cut a good lot of pumpkin into bite-sized pieces, roughly cut up an onion or two and some garlic, and mix the lot together with olive oil in a baking dish. Bake.

Sprinkle with salt, tamari, toasted sesame seed oil and a squeeze of lemon juice when done. Throw in some chopped up spring onion if you have any (a great colour ingredient).

All Seasons Vegie Pie

Mix together: three cups of any half-cooked vegies in season, 3 or 4 eggs, a bit of leftover grain or pasta if you have any (but not necessary), a cup of SR flour and 1/3 cup of oil. Then add salt, pepper and any flavourings you want.

Slop into a baking or pie dish (about 3 to 4 cm deep) and bake. Yumscious hot or cold. It's a manageable pie/slice to tote around in a packed lunch and eat with fingers later on too.

Variations on a Cob Oven

One way to learn about earth ovens is to build and use a series. Here Dunja, now planning her third wood-fired oven, describes the basic process and muses on future refinements.

by Dunja Kuhr

FRANKLINFORD, VICTORIA

WHAT is it about cob ovens that fuels our imagination, makes us feel at home, and gives us comfort? It must be a genetic memory that gives us the message of 'home and safe' somehow, and allows us to gather around, relax and cook within the earth.

It is a cold end-of-summer day out there and here I sit pondering on cob oven versions one and two, while planning version three to be built soon. Will it be a "make a cob oven in a day and eat pizza that night" or a three-day version? It won't matter — I'll still love it!

Version 1 —the Wombat

This cob oven was cute and small (one pizza), and we built it one winter afternoon in 1999 in a four-person workshop led by our friends Don and Sue. It was built around a slice of timber as a door. While we were building our strawbale cottage, however, it fell victim to the weather, my wild nephews (over-firing the poor thing until it cracked) and finally an out-of-control Bobcat reversing while installing the pond. Well, it was in the wrong spot anyhow: the strawbale garden seats later took this piece of ground.

Version 2 — built winter 2000

Our friends Khane and Karmen wanted to come up for the weekend and help build version two — sure, the more, the merrier! I had already prepared the site with four posts for a roof this time and the required materials were on hand.

Materials

A rock base made from large bluestones (excavated by the tonne during water treatment system installation), small gaps filled with crushed rock, a steel frame hammered into the base for the two old stove doors we had found, flat bricks, sand, and fine sand, and of course pre-soaked buckets of clay and a large bag of chopped straw. We also had some builder's plastic, some thin plastic and a cement mixer.

The set Saturday came. Roland was as sick as a dog. Our friends arrived around lunchtime and Khane looked no better: they must have had the same virus, which they then tried the rest of the day to cure with lots of beer.

Karmen and I were ready to roll and we started making cob while the boys set the bricks on a bed of fine sand in a sort of level fashion, filling the spaces between the bricks with more fine white sand.

We girls loaded the mixer with sand and added (while sieving out little rocks) the slurried clay. Simply pre-soak clay in large buckets for a day or two, then mix with shovel or a mixing blade welded to a rod, powered by your electric drill. (We had the latter which was faster, yet I began to render with the shovel and it works too: just soak as long as you can, here and there stirring it through). We then transferred the mix onto the plastic sheet until we had enough to start cobbing.

The cobbing

You'll need three layers of cob. The first layer is just sand and clay only, the second is the same with straw mixed into it, and the third is sand with a little clay only. When we had a few mixer loads (say three to four wheelbarrows), we began making little cobs. This can be fairly high in clay content: sticky but not too wet. When is it right? What you want is a mix that you can pick up and throw because that comes next. Pick up small handfuls of the stuff, shape into a ball and throw it back and forth a few times. Collect it in a wheelbarrow or throw it to the laying crew if you have lots of helpers to put it straight on.

Progress

The day was getting on and two carloads of Khane's friends rolled up to have a stickybeak at the cottage in progress while they were visiting Daylesford for the weekend.

"And what the hell are you doing there?"

Well, lots of talk, more beer, a fire to sit around, but not in the oven yet. If you don't use the ready little cobs or pre-made cob mixture immediately, then moisten and cover them, THEN sit down for a chat. Khane, however, still got the lump of sand onto the base, which became the formwork for the next stage, tomorrow.

Sunday

I shaped the sand lump that forms the mould for the cob, and we covered it with thin plastic. This stops the cob sticking to the sand and makes removal of the sand later much easier. Avoid large folds and thick plastic as the cob has a tendency to catch underneath the fold and rip the foil or damage the layers as you remove it.

Dunya applies the first layer evenly, leaving fingerprints and dents as a key for the next layer.

Next we started to cob up the oven with our pre-made cobs. Remember that you have three layers, and leave clearance around the doors. Start at the bottom door end and work around the base and upwards. If you use a timber door (version one) set it in place and cob around it, remembering that you will want it tight but need to remove it without breaking the layers.

Simply place your cobs onto the base, keep adding, and pound and knead them to each other with your fingers as you continue (ever made sausage-rolled clay pots in school?). Cover the entire oven trying to somehow keep an even thickness and leaving fingerprints and dents and grooves if you like. This 'keying' will then make the next layer adhere better. Make allowance for your vent hole and leave it free. Ours is at the back and top of the oven, yet this may change in version three.

This really is a nice job and very relaxing if you're not working with the virally-infected.

Second coat

When you're finished, add the second coat. We girls started mixing chopped straw into the leftover mix on the groundsheet (a whipper snipper and garden mulcher are great for chopping). To mix thoroughly, we stomped on the mix, rolled the sheet back and forwards by lifting each side and folding the mix again and again while adding more straw.

It should hold together nicely and the force of catching will compress or 'de-air' the mix. Again, collect the cobs in a wheelbarrow or throw them straight to the laying crew. Lay them as previously, making sure of a good bond to the base coat.

Monday

Today I used the pre-made straw, sand, and clay cobs and cobbed up the second coat. If you like decorations make shapes around the vent hole, and doors (eyes and ears?). Then I revved up the mixer again and made another load of mix for the cobs of the final coat. This time no straw and finer sand if you have any. This layer should be a more sandy mix: just add enough clay slurry to hold the mix together.

Less clay means less cracking, and better protection.

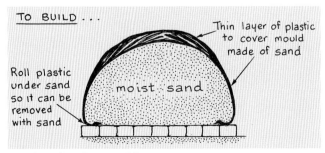

Section showing sand form.

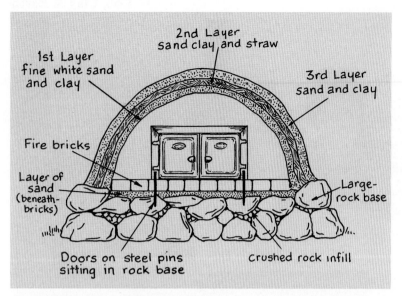

Cross section through base and layers.

(Labels in diagram:)
1st Layer fine white sand and clay
2nd Layer sand clay and straw
3rd Layer sand and clay
Fire bricks
Layer of sand (beneath-bricks)
Large-rock base
Doors on steel pins sitting in rock base
Crushed rock infill

As there was no straw to be added I formed the cobs straight out of the barrow and pounded them between my hands a little to remove trapped air. Then I cobbed up the third layer like the others, making sure that I maintained a good bond.

I let the oven dry for the rest of the week and then started to remove the sand inside which had acted as a form.

All went well in the beginning but I found that the oven was very deep and my arms pretty short and the door too narrow for my humble shape: I never thought of that one! I used small garden shovels carefully so not to hit the side or back wall, and Roland finally turned up with his much longer arm reach — and no virus … Godsend! Luckily, no cob had stuck to the plastic liner and we removed it easily. Pizza time!

Eighteen months later

The oven has a roof and partial walls (some 'stickcover' to the north and east). We had a few fierce storms and I found that the third coat is starting to wear from the driving rain (west, which has no cover). Some cracks appear on the surface but none have gone right through the approximately four to five-centimetre-thick layer. As the unsealed third coat of our strawbale cottage has also been affected by this western exposure I will re-render this side before winter. Then I will add another layer of cob to the oven and maybe trial a lime render/wash which Don and Sue have just added to their own cob oven.

Version three

We are building again — another strawbale

Below: eighteen months later the oven has some wear and a few surface cracks.

RECIPES

Sourdough Starter

Day 1. Place 100 g wholemeal flour with 125 ml warm water in a high bowl (best of clay), mix and cover with cloth.

Day 2. Add 100 g w/m flour and 125 ml warm water, mix and cover with cloth.

Day 3. Add 200 g w/m flour and 250 ml warm water, mix and cover with cloth.

No guarantees — the mix will rise and foam high so make the bowl high! It will smell sour and may attract vinegar flies. Keep all on a sunny windowsill or near a heater or other warm spot.

Sourdough Bread

1kg w/m flour

1 portion of sourdough starter

About 3/4 litre warm water per mixing step/day

Salt 4 tsp

Spices, grains — sunflower, sesame, wheat germ, oats, linseed ... (I use 3–4 handfuls)

Step1 (I do this in the morning)

In a large high bowl mix s/d starter with the half litre warm water. Add 500 g or a bit more than 1/2 the packet of flour.

Mix well with wooden spoon. Possibly add another 1/4 cup warm water. Dough should be not too thick. Leave, approx. 12 hrs, in a warm spot covered with aluminium foil and cloth. Dough must not dry out.

Step 2 (next day — I do this at night)

Take off next starter culture (approx. 500 ml, cover and store in fridge (will keep for about two months, may then be a little lame).

Add to bowl the rest of the packet of flour (3 1/3 cups, 500 g), 1/2 litre warm water, salt, grains and secret herbs and spices ... Maybe add more water? (I use about 3/4 litre for mine).

Fill mix equally into two greased (oil spray) bread tins.

I let this stand, still covered, for a bit over an hour for the bread to rise.

Then remove foil and bake at 180–200°C for an hour.

Since I now don't have an oven with temp gauge I guess — medium to hot. Somewhere in the red section — higher at first. In the cob-oven ditto.

This is really YUM!!! Gifted to me some 15 years ago by Doris, a friend from Berlin who fed this bread for many years (she mixed rye and wholemeal flours) to her family.

house of course, but this time for us to live in rather than to rent to visitors. In front of the caravan (our present shelter and later to become the wwoofers'/ visitors' quarters) I have the bases for two very large strawbale seats, which will be rendered in earth/lime render this time. They have severe weather exposure and are to be the test for our house render. There will also be another cob oven near these seats. This time it will be a little different.

The base will be much higher, about waist height. This makes access much easier for firing and getting food in and out — much more user-friendly. I am still looking for an easy way (I like it simple as no engineering degree is in my pocket) to also create a space underneath for wood storage. Maybe extra large rocks in mortar as a rim, more mortar to a level top, then a 10 mm steel plate, then another layer of rock for the base as previously? Any other ideas? I am searching for some actual firebricks (not just fired bricks) as used for kilns and the like for the base. They should retain the heat better and cook the food more efficiently from underneath.

We shall follow Roland's idea of placing the vent hole to the top at the front. His theory is that the oven draws from the door and then the heat will curl around the base and top and will circulate better if vented at the front — I will let you know.

Depending on the lime render trial I will give the oven a final lime coat to weather-protect it. Any helpers? Version four will then end up being made in our outside area when the house is finished. What will it be?

Willows Muse strawbale cottage can be booked by phoning Dunja on (03) 5476 4445, fax (03) 5476 4429, or email <dunatdac@netcon.net.au>.

General Notes

- Avoid metal tools.
- If on occasion the dough above becomes lame I add a sprinkle of dry yeast or a few crumbles of fresh yeast to the s/d in the first step.
- For a change, roast onion slices or pumpkin, and add on day two the secret herbs and spices.
- Will keep moist for almost a week if stored in a paper bag or similar.

Earth Oven Southern Italian Style

This earth oven features some interesting and useful extra options. Henk and Helma tell how they added to their oven using some attractive recycled materials.

by Henk and Helma Bak

TRENTHAM, VICTORIA

The posts of the shelter and table are of quartered fallen hardwood. Slate tabletops and paving were also sourced locally.

O N THE EDGE of township, farming land and the Wombat Forest, our property 'Evera' is on 15 acres of former grazing land, which we are developing into a private park. *Evera* means spring, and implies renewal and a spiritual dimension in education, crafts and ecology (ecosophy) through camps, seminars and working bees.

During our first three camps we had simple projects going: a sandpit, a set of swings, a cubby house, a play. For the fourth camp we invited our friends Anna and John Rando, from Officer (near Pakenham), as artist/craftspeople-in-residence. Their specialty is in building earth ovens and making utensils for them. We asked them to build one for us and with us. Here we try to share what we learnt.

Preparation: We got most of the materials to John's specification: sand, bricks, rocks and slate; he brought clay from their land and a hand-crafted wooden door.

Position: As the oven was a community concern, we decided on a place on the land, against the backdrop of a stand of trees, rather than close to house and kitchen.

Foundation: A 3.3 x 3.3 m area was levelled for paving and base. The base is 1.9 m wide, 1.15 m deep and 0.87 m high, built of rocks. The oven floor is paved with old red bricks. Five bricks side by side form the sill for the opening. To the left of the oven the base forms a platform, topped with slate.

Oven: We started the wall with a circular row of small half-dried mud bricks, and then made a mould for the dome with moist sand, using a template. This, then, was covered with newspaper. The mud dome was built over this mould. Mud bricks and wall were made from slow-drying clay, mixed with some gravel and straw. The oven floor is 1.05 m above the ground. Height of dome: 0.80 m. Diameter inside: 1.10 m. A template helped shape the opening for the door, 38 cm wide, 37 cm high. Airholes were opened in the wall, 15 cm from base and 4 cm in diameter: one at the back, one on each side.

Protective structure: As we had some rain during the building process, we placed an old, large, heavy canvas tent over it. For permanent protection, we later built a simple structure: two 2.7 m posts in front, two 2.0 m posts at back, on a 3 m x 3 m area, with a roof covered with tiles. The (critical!) distance between oven door and roof is 0.90 m. We placed the structure over the oven so that we can store firewood behind it. To keep out rain and still maintain the transparency of the whole, we used corrugated see-through roofing material plus a trellis as back wall.

Additional equipment: For preparing food we built a table with granite top inside the structure. In the immediate environment we placed moveable items: a brazier, to hold the burning fuel when baking starts; a sink; a garden table and benches; and a wooden container for storing kitchen utensils and crockery. For tools we got a flattish spade and a garden scraper, both with long handles, and on the occasion of the first firing, at Easter 2004, John presented us with a flat, wooden, handmade scoop, called a 'peel', whilst Anna brought her homemade pizza: more delicious than anyone had ever tasted!

Use: John and Anna prefer to call it an earth oven rather than a pizza oven, as, indeed, the oven is just as well used for baking bread, frying meat, toasting, roasting, and even firing pottery (leaving the fuel in). It takes about two and a half hours to heat up and stays hot enough to bake, fry and cook for at least four hours. The door is only used when the burning fuel has

Henk displays the charred inside surface of the heavy timber door.

been taken out. Every firing is a social event: very engaging, people preparing, conversing; and everything gets an intensely satisfying nourishing flavour. We use the best ingredients, bio-dynamic or organic, but the wood fire makes them even more special. The baking time is remarkably short.

Maintenance: With the proper protective roof over it, there is little maintenance needed: the skin of the dome might crack a bit, but providing one uses the same slow-drying clay, there is no problem. Most of the black at the entrance of the oven can be brushed away with soap and smoothed over with some fresh clay.

Right from the start the project generated much interest and involvement as well as a fascination to watch John and Anna working and explaining along the way. The kids loved the mudbrick making. The adults couldn't keep their hands off the puzzle of shaping the base with irregular rocks. Just as challenging was

The clay for the dome and mudbricks came from the town of Officer by courtesy of John and Anna Rando.

the paving of the floor around the base after the camp by women friends.

As a finishing touch, recycled iron curly braces were mounted to the front posts and architrave. Our son Tao examined it from the distance and offered his verdict: "Leunig would approve!"

Permaculture Mixed With Cob Oven

Naomi explains how earth ovens can have a social function and can be used as an indoor heating source, as well being a great way to cook food.

by Naomi Coleman

SOUTHERN CROSS PERMACULTURE INSTITUTE,
LEONGATHA SOUTH, VICTORIA

AFTER 13 years implementing our permaculture demonstration site, we are at a stage where we can slow down on the hard work and start to spend more time on the luxuries of life. We had talked about having a cob oven for cooking on our permaculture courses for a while. When our two intern teachers wanted to run their first workshop independently, we were happy to hand over the task. In true permaculture style we used human biological resources and our Cob Oven Building Workshop was held in May 2006. Learning the ancient craft of building a simple functional outdoor oven with a good group of people, good music, excellent food shared and reasonable weather meant a great weekend for all.

Cob ovens are a low cost, low impact way of creating an alternative cooking source and provide an attractive focal point for community gatherings and family dinners. We decided to build ours in our big shed, as we are slowly turning this area into an outdoor entertaining area, and it's near the kitchen, and has lights for night use. A couple of potential areas were analysed, but in the end the shed won out as it is a covered area. In Leongatha, where even in a drought year we get 700 mm of rain, a cob oven needs protection. We plan to use the oven on our PDC courses, parties and to heat the shed in winter.

Cam and Sarah constructed the rock base first with local materials. Underneath the oven, within the rock base, is a wood storage area, although the kids like it as a cubby! Then a reinforced concrete base was laid using formwork, ready for the workshop to start. We had nine participants come along to learn the craft of cob oven building, and the oven was built in a weekend.

We used a local mud that we had used for building our mudbrick classroom. This already had a good mix of clay and sand as required for maximum strength with minimum shrinkage. The first layer, the thermal layer, is constructed using pure clay and sand, about 75 mm thick. The mixing process requires good music, as you literally have to throw your shoes off, jump in, and do the twist!

To lay the cob, throw the cob from hand to hand, and whack it, ensuring it is a good consistency, and then make little bricks. These are laid one on top of the other, scoring each to ensure a good bond, and making sure you push back down onto the cob, rather than into your beautiful sand dome which will distort if you knock it around too much.

Cam packs sand on the rock and cement base, ready to lay the firebricks.

The dome is later removed and is the cavity in which beautiful pizzas, roasts, breads, yoghurts and whatever else you like will be made.

To the second insulating layer, which is around 150 mm thick, straw is added for insulation and to give the mix strength, acting like reo mesh in concrete. This layer can be packed on in chunks, pushing the mix into itself to remove any air gaps. Once finished, to get it nice and smooth, hit it nice and hard with a plank.

After drying off for a couple of months, large cracks did start to appear. Closures at the local quarry meant there was little time for pre-building testing, which is highly recommended. It's no problem though, we just applied rolled bits of cob and compressed them into the cracks, making sure we wet the area first so that the new mud would bond. After three months and a firing, the oven has not cracked further, and this weekend we will have our first cook up when we cook pizzas for 26 students. Cam has returned to take on the role of chef this time — we promised we'd wait for him to fire it up the first time, and we look forward to the results.

Thanks to all the participants who helped create the oven and to Cam Wilson and Sarah Massey for running the workshop.

The first layer is scored to help bond the second layer, with nails marking the door. Below: Naomi in front of the cob oven with the new door inserted.

Building the 'Ups 'n' Downs' Cob Oven

Easy, fast and economical to build, Dorothy and Harry's cob oven stimulated the creative juices as well as the digestive ones.

by Dorothy and Harry Creevey

OLD BONALBO, NEW SOUTH WALES

Young and old mix the cob to a techno beat.

OUR decision to build an earth oven stemmed from requests, permaculture ideology, and a desire to prove that something unique, practical and beautiful could be created for next to nothing, and provide great bonding and fun in its creation.

Building a cob oven is like taking a step back in time, back to your childhood when you felt free to build sandcastles and make mud pies, or even to a more primitive time.

Building in mud provides tribal bonding, as anyone from toddlers to great-grandma can participate and artistic members can let their imagination run wild. Puddling mud will find the kids squealing with glee, and after a few tentative minutes, even clean freaks are infected with the call of the mud. As they take their first tentative poke at the mud and feel its silkiness ooze up between their toes, they are hooked!

In no time at all protective gloves and footwear are discarded as young and old perform the cob twist (techno music required).

On a more practical level, cob was chosen for our oven as it is easy and fast to build and the materials were available on site or nearby.

Only basic tools are required and generally even these tools are quickly discarded as you discover it's easier to pick up handfuls of clay than shovel it, and hands do a better job than a trowel and that it's more fun, and helps to de-air the cob, if loaves are thrown down a people chain, instead of using a wheelbarrow.

Our preferred design was the traditional dome and as we aren't getting any younger, it is on a raised platform. Reject rocks from

The insulation layer was 30:70 sand and clay, and as much straw as it would hold.

RECIPES

Damper

Equipment:

Large bowl and sieve

20 cm cake pan

- Allow the cob oven's flames to die down to hot coals
- Cook for approx. 20 minutes
- Suitable to follow pizzas

Ingredients

4 cups SR flour

60 g butter

1 cup water

1 tsp salt

1 level tbsp honey or sugar

Instructions

1. Pre-heat cob oven
2. Sift dry ingredients.
3. Rub in butter.
4. Pour water into flour well.
5. Mix into a soft dough.
6. Empty out onto a floured surface and knead lightly.
7. Place rounded side up in pan
8. Cook about 20 minutes.
9. Serve hot with butter, honey, syrup, jam.

Damper — Wheat-free

Ingredients

4 cups wheat flour substitute

4 tsp gluten-free baking powder

60 g butter

1 cup water

1 tsp salt

1 level tbsp sugar

Instructions

As wheat flour damper

Spinach Pie

Ingredients

1 quantity of savoury pastry such as shortcrust, uncooked

4–6 eggs, depending on size

1 cup natural yoghurt or kefir

1/2 cup fetta cheese, grated

Herbs of choice: oregano, celery seed, thyme, rosemary, parsley

2/3 cup cheese, grated (can be mix of block, mozzarella and/or parmesan)

1–2 cups spinach or silverbeet or warrigal greens or poor man's spinach, or a mixture — cooked until wilted, strained (discard water), chopped and cooled

Method

1. Line dish with pastry.
2. Whisk eggs and yoghurt well together.
3. Mix in cheese/s (reserve some of the cheese (not fetta) for topping).
4. Mix in the spinach and herbs.
5. Pour into pastry case and top with a sprinkling of cheese.
6. Cook until set in a moderate oven (suitable for a cob oven).

Wheat-free Savoury Pastry

Ingredients

3 cups wheat-free flour

2 tsp baking powder

1 egg, lightly beaten

2 tbsp olive oil

Approx. 2 tbsp hot water or as needed

Instructions

1. Sift flour and baking powder and make a well.
2. Mix in the egg and the oil.
3. Add enough hot water to make a pastry.
4. Roll out or press into dish.
5. Either blind bake or brush with egg white and add filling.
6. Reduce wheat flour pastry cooking temperature by 20°C and increase baking time.

Dorothy and Harry used three different render compositions on their large oven.

a neighbour's quarry provided the platform's outer wall and the centre was filled with sand and rubble for thermal mass. Bricks laid in a sand-bed formed the oven floor. At 1000 mm diameter and with the internal oven height around 600 mm, it is a large oven. An oven door and ashtray vent from a discarded stove was resurrected as the oven door and adjustable air vent. The door sits in place and the vent is mudded in over a pre-formed vent hole at the back.

A sandcastle of damp sand was built as a mould and wrapped in plastic before a firebox cob layer of 70:30 sand and clay was laid over it. When this was 'greenhide' dry, an insulation layer of 30:70 sand and clay, and as much straw as it would hold, was added.

Again at 'greenhide' dry, render was applied for added appeal and some weather protection. For interest, and to separate the different renders I wanted to experiment with, the snake relief was created. The white render is lime, the grey, dung, and the red is clay. Of these my personal preference is the dung.

Any cracking after drying was grouted with render.

For added weather protection a discarded rainwater tank was cut in half and rested on posts and rails as a roof.

Puddling was done on a sheet of plastic and the materials used were sand from our property and discarded clay dug from a dam wall to allow the dam to be fenced. Straw was used as the fibre content.

The only costs involved have been the cement for mortar, lime for the lime render, and a bale of straw. All of these could have been replaced with available free materials. Mud mortar could just as easily been used and all of the render could have been mud or dung. Water weed or Lomandra lily leaves could have replaced the straw.

As the oven is large and the walls 20 to 30 centimetres thick, it takes about two hours to reach cooking temperature. A single firing can easily cater for 40 people within two hours, and will continue to cook for about eight hours.

To maximise energy use, we cook dishes requiring a hot oven like pizzas first, followed by bread, pies, cakes, quiche and use residual heat to toast muesli and dry produce. It cooks surprisingly quickly with pizzas taking two to three minutes and a damper in 10 to 20 minutes.

If re-fired next morning, it is ready for cooking in around an hour.

It is a shining example of how practical beauty can be created with locally available, cheap or free resources, a few simple tools and lots of fun.

As for enjoying your creation: can you think of a better way to spend quality time with friends or family than sitting around the oven as it cooks not only this meal, but tomorrow's bread and quiche before toasting the muesli for breakfast? And being mesmerised by dancing flames or dying embers is much more therapeutic than sitting around the campfire equivalent of today, the television, where violence reigns supreme.

Enjoy creating and using your oven, and why stop there now you have the bug? Perhaps this unique landscaping feature could be accompanied with cob seats, a cob garden wall and ...?

Thanks all who participated in its creation.

From Earth Garden to Pizza Oven

This simple clay oven looks good and has been the centre of some great evenings with friends. As Philip explains, his approach was by the book.

by Philip Drew,
COLAC, VICTORIA

The clay dome is about 18 cm thick: a great thermal mass for cooking.

I WAS first inspired to build an earth oven after reading an article in *Earth Garden*. I contacted the author via the *Earth Garden* office to find out how best to build an oven. The author of the article emailed me details of Kiko Denzer's book *Build Your Own Earth Oven**. The next question was how to get a copy of this book. Internet searches proved unsatisfactory. Surprisingly, there was a copy in our local library. I followed Denzer's instructions almost to the 'T'.

I made the base from old house bricks, which I'd cut the corners off (with an angle grinder) to allow them to sit in a tighter circle. These base bricks are held in place by the weight of the dome. I filled the inside of the base with the cut brick corners and other waste rubble. This was topped with sand from an old sandpit and watered in to fill the gaps between the rubble. Next, I purchased the firebricks for the oven floor, the most costly part of the oven, about $90. In hindsight, I might have used less expensive old house bricks, flat side up, but the firebricks do give up their heat and cook quickly. Sand from the sandpit was formed for the shape of the inner dome. Suitable clay came from a friend who had recently done some excavating on his farm. His wife came to enjoy a ceremonial patting of the mud as I began the several hours' work. I had followed the book's advice, placing newspaper on the surface of the sand mould so I'd know when the sand stopped and the clay began when later removing the inner sand.

The clay dome was completed in three stages (inner, middle and outer layer), as suggested, about a week apart, and is now about 18 cm thick: a great thermal mass for cooking. My clay work? Having the right consistency could definitely be improved, but the actual shaping of it, slopping it on and forming the walls was great. The top layer cracked too much as it dried so I replaced it three times before I was happy with the straw/sand/clay mix. I may have been too impatient to let the intermediate layer dry well enough. A few big cracks have developed over time, but the overall integrity of the oven is fine and these cracks acted a bit like mini chimneys. It still looks good. I'll patch them soon.

I made a wooden plug door, lined with tin, to fit the oven opening but ended up not using it as much as I expected, only when I scrape the coals back over the firebricks to reheat them before the fifth and sixth pizzas go in. A local steel fabricator put my oven shovel/scraper together for a reasonable cost. I use this for pushing coals around inside the oven and for cleaning ash when finished. After searching the internet, I found out that the big spatula used in pizza ovens was called a 'peel'. I found a shop in Geelong which sold me one for only $11; the peel has proved invaluable and looks impressive.

It takes about three hours to fire up the oven. I know it's ready when I can comfortably feel the warmth with my hand on the outside. At this stage, the inside is full of red coals (hardwoods are best). To cook, I push the coals around the edge and place the pizza in the middle of the firebrick floor. I originally thought that it would be big enough for two or three pizzas to cook at once, but not so. Because the cooking is so quick (the first pizza cooks in about two minutes), there was enough pizza continually coming out of the oven to satisfy the hunger of sizable gatherings. We have had some great evenings with guests putting their preferred pizza together for all to share. A 'Pizza-off' is the name given to our competition for the best pizza. (I won this once with my yabbie, garlic, bacon and olive combination).

I found the project hard work but fun and definitely worth it. Its' pleasing shape looks attractive all year round. Good luck with yours.

*This book is now available from the Good Life Book Club. Four ways to order: MAIL: PO Box 2, Trentham, Victoria, 3458. FAX: (03) 5424 1743 EMAIL: goodlife@earthgarden.com.au or visit www.goodlifebookclub.com PHONE: (03) 5424 1814.

Very satisfied workshoppers, ready to go home and start on their own backyard ovens.

Alan Watt's Workshops

Alan Watt has been running oven-building workshops for many years all over south-east Australia. He builds low-tech earth/clay ovens, high-tech refractory cement ovens, and superb-looking brick ovens. *Earth Garden* editor, Alan T Gray attended one of Alan's recent workshops and explains what he did and what he learned.

by Alan T Gray
TRENTHAM, VICTORIA

MY FAMILY and I have often daydreamed about a wood-fired backyard oven so when I saw an oven-making workshop advertised at the Lavandula Farm and café near Daylesford I quickly wrote down the phone number and stuck it on my computer screen. Six months later I was lucky enough to get a place on the November '06 weekend workshop run by Alan Watt, a friendly and knowledgeable former head of the Ceramics Department of the Art School at ANU.

Alan ran a well-organised weekend, supervising 16 of us to build three types of ovens: a 'low-tech' earth oven, a 'high-tech' oven made of high temperature 'castable', and a super-fancy 'beehive-shaped' brick oven.

The first two ovens were built on steel tables that Alan had welded up before the workshop began and were destined to be transported to new homes' after the workshop. The brick oven was built on a besser block and concrete base, so the lucky hosts of the workshop (Alan's daughter and son-in-law) got to retain the oven at the end of the weekend.

After an initial lecture by Alan, people gravitated to help build the oven that interested them most. These allegiances shifted slightly over the course of the weekend and I found myself infatuated with the low-tech, earth oven. In fact, I liked it so much I bought it!

Bricks and pavers
On the first morning we learned how to create the thermal oven base. For permanent, higher tech ovens like the brick Taj Mahal we were tackling, the first layer on top of the concrete base should be a compacted decomposed granite fill, screeded to a level surface, ready for the thermal base of firebrick tiles or bricks. On the low-tech oven we used ceramic pavers, such as the Austral brand 'Bowral' pavers — Alan has found these to be ideal and much cheaper than the firebrick tiles.

For brick ovens standard fire bricks are generally recommended but as Alan pointed out these are capable of withstanding 1400°C – an overkill for an oven that would rarely reach 650°. He recommended, and we used, a common solid cream house brick, cut in half (about a quarter the price of fire bricks).

A white brick will generally take greater heat than a red one, so if you're going to use house bricks to build

The costs of building a refractory cement oven on the left, and a low-tech cob oven on the right.

THE COB OVEN

1. The half-pear shape of the cob oven interior is formed with a ring of pavers.

2. The sand mould is covered with a painter's drop sheet.

3. Lumps of clay are crushed and sieved.

4. Mixing the clay, sand and chopped sisal fibre.

5. The sand (and foam box) can now be slowly removed.

6. To test if your clay mix is the right consistency, form it into a 'sausage' and bend it over your finger. 7. The mix should 'bend' before it breaks. If it bends right round your finger, it's too plastic. If it breaks before it starts to bend, it's too brittle. 8. Brendan removes some exquisite loaves of olive bread.   Above: a very happy owner cooks his first pizza in his new cob oven.

your own backyard oven, go for the old cream bricks.

On top of the steel frame or tables Alan had fitted a layer of aerated 'Hebel' blocks which are ideal insulators. This was a substitute for the 'heat-bank' of decomposed granite which would have made the 'transportable' ovens extremely heavy to lift and shift.

We then used a light coating of air-setting high temperature mortar to bond the Austral pavers to the Hebel layer. Next we formed the oval perimeter of the inside of the ovens with a course of pavers mortared on their sides. This 'skirt' provided a vertical, hard surface which would withstand the constant bumping of the oven broom when cleaning the floor of coals and ash. A gap was left at the front for the wooden formwork which Alan supplied to create the doorway.

After a break for morning tea and more lectures from Alan we were ready to form the sand mould which would give us the classic dome shape of the oven. The idea is to form a sand mould and apply the oven material to this, eventually removing the sand through the open doorway so you're left with

a domed oven. It sounds simple and — with Alan's expert guidance — it was.

First we placed a styrene foam box in the oven to save space, and then covered this with brickie's sand as we moulded the final shape of the oven interior.

Next we covered the sand mould with a painter's plastic drop sheet: this ensures that the sand will come away easily from inside the oven and not be bonded to the oven building material.

Oven temperatures

Alan interspersed the hands-on work with regular discussions to teach us about the finer aspects of understanding these ovens. In the initial heating up the air temperature inside a wood-fired oven can get to around 600°C – the temperature at which carbon (the black soot on the apex of the oven) will burn away. The bricks on the base, meanwhile, can get to a massive 900°C. But this is still well short of the 1100°C that clay house bricks or clay pavers are fired at. This explains, for economic reasons, why Alan recommends normal

THE BRICK OVEN

1. The brick oven base ready for the granite fill.

2. Workshop leader Alan Watt with the guide for the brick oven's sand mould.

3. The finished sand mould: next step is the bricklaying.

4. Close to finishing all the bricking.

5. The sand mould has been removed, the flue pipe is in place and the steel needles are clearly visible in the mortar.

cream house bricks for building a brick oven.

High temperature castable

Standard builders' concrete is a mixture of cement, stone and sand but as this would break down over 300°C it is unsuitable for oven building.

A high temperature concrete known simply as 'castable' is used for higher temperatures and is made from a high alumina cement plus an aggregate of highly siliceious stone and/or ground ceramic material.

This pre-mix refractory material was used in the high-tech oven and as a coating on the brick oven. One brand of castable made in Sydney also has fine synthetic fibres mixed throughout to aid workability.

On the high-tech oven we applied an initial layer of castable 10 mm thick. In the second layer

The brick door frame and steel hinged doorway are in place as the sand mould is completed.

The first layer of refractory cement goes on top of the painter's drop sheet.

we also mixed through some stainless steel 'needles' to act as reinforcing – the furnace maker's equivalent of reo mesh in a concrete slab.

Clay for the low-tech oven

Meanwhile, over at the low-tech work area, we were getting down and dirty with pounding and sieving lumps of recently dug bright yellow clay through an old bed base. For every 1/3 barrowload of finely sieved clay we'd add the same quantity of brickie's sand and some fine stone (crushed bluestone), and some short lengths of sisal rope fibre — the low tech equivalent of the stainless steel 'needles'.

Kneading the clay into large, even balls was one of the least rivetting parts of the weekend — but it had to be done. In teams of five, we squatted over wooden boards and kneaded as you would a lovely loaf of sourdough bread. Every now and then, we'd break off half our kneaded clay and pass it on to the kneader next in the circle, while accepting some of our neighbour's ball. This, Alan assured us, meant a very evenly mixed batch of clay ready for the next, vital step.

Now came the most fun for the day: taking a tennis ball-sized lump of clay and flattening it to make a pancake about 15 mm thick. We then placed this pancake on top of the sand mould connecting with our neighbours' pancakes until the sand mould was completely covered. After three layers of clay to a total thickness of about 45 mm, with more packed in around Alan's wooden door mould, we had the makings of an oven.

Alan carefully fitted the metal chimney pipe into the front of the oven above the doorway so we could keep building up layers of clay around it.

Eventually we had a very impressive-looking earth oven, a high-tech oven covered in high temperature castable with a fancy brick doorway and matching steel

door, and a brick oven that was looking like it needed a lot more hours before an edible pizza would emerge. It was clear that the higher-tech the oven, the more hours work it would take to build — pretty obvious really.

Day Two

On our second morning we arrived to find that Alan had been working throughout the night speeding up the natural drying process of the clay oven by gradually removing the sand and foam box support inside the oven.

As the sand mould was removed through the door in slow stages Alan would place a small gas burner beneath the exposed clay dome and gently heat the oven to dry it. Normally this would dry naturally over a few days or weeks, if covered, but it is important to remove the sand before the clay dries and shrinks.

His 'speed drying' of the oven was to satisfy our impatience to try out the oven even though it was only partially complete!

The castable high tech oven had set nicely overnight and we could now remove the sand mould and start applying a layer of insulating material: a high-tech ceramic fibre blanket that will effectively hold in the heat.

The brick oven was also progressing well: after finishing the sand mould and cutting the cream bricks to size, we were ready to mortar them in place. Of course, we were able to build up layers of bricks that created a perfect beehive shape, using the sand mould to support each brick end in place so that it was wedged in by its neighbour and couldn't collapse into the oven centre: an ancient and clever building method!

Alan discussed pizza making, tools, and cooking methods over morning tea, and we built up the fire in the clay oven that had been started earlier in the morning. Now we were ready to apply the low-tech

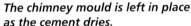

The chimney mould is left in place as the cement dries.

Happy owners about to apply the final colour render coats.

insulating coats to the clay oven. This consists of a mixture of sawmill sawdust, and clay mixed with water to a fairly dry consistency. We applied this with our hands to the hot oven: steam rose instantly as the layers dried and the sawdust in the inner layers was 'cooked', to leave tiny air pockets to form our low-tech insulating coat.

While we applied these coats, we also started cooking: scones, focaccias and bread. It seemed too good to be true — we were cooking already and the oven was only partially finished!

Final coats

Now we were flying along. The bricking was finished on the brick oven, and a covering coat of mortar was applied to pretty it up. Meanwhile, it was time for the final coats on the high-tech and low-tech (clay) ovens. This was simpler than I'd imagined: on the clay oven two brushable coats of clay and water, mixed to the consistency of pancake batter, and then a final coat of clay and water, with a dash of Bondcrete added to the mix for weatherproofing. At this stage you can add oxides to your 'paint' mix if you have a particular colour in mind. Hey presto — there's your oven.

The high tech oven was also 'painted' with a similar final coat but in this case it was a standard cement/sand render with colouring oxides added.

Proof's in the eating

It's hard to explain how satisfying it was to take the next step: Brendan, one of our number, is a professional baker and had whipped up a dough base for about 30 pizza bases. Alan provided pizza trays and ingredients, and we all pitched in to make our own pizza toppings. Oil the tray, spread the dough and 'top' to your heart's content.

Brendan kindly agreed to wield the pizza peel and within a few minutes there were two pizzas side by side cooking in the clay oven. They were undoubtedly the best pizzas we'd ever tasted.

The fire

Alan recommends firing your oven for two hours before cooking. I was amazed how little firewood he used to get the oven up to cooking temperature. Just before we were ready to cook we pushed the fire to the back of the oven. This left a stinking hot oven base, and massive amounts of heat radiating back into the middle of the oven from all points inside the domed oven. As Alan said: "We build a domed oven because flames hate corners."

The surprising thing for me was that this fire had been run for two hours with very small amounts of firewood — each piece no thicker than my thumb.

After about 30 pizzas, and three loaves of olive bread made by Brendan, we could say that the workshop oven was a huge success. The castable oven was near completion as the final waterproof coat was applied, and the brick oven had the 'ceramic blanket' insulation added and its stainless steel 'needle' coat applied before the end of the day, so it was very close to finished as well.

This was a superb workshop because Alan knew exactly how to run it so that everyone felt included, but more importantly everyone came away knowledgeable and enthusiastic about building their own. You couldn't hope to do a more satisfying oven-building workshop.

• *For details about Alan's forthcoming oven workshops visit his website at:www.woodfiredovenworkshops. com, email him at woodfiredovenworkshops@bigpond .com or phone Alan on (02) 6494 0015.*

Back Yard Bliss

You've built the oven, now how do you use it? *Earth Garden* editor, Alan T Gray, describes his family's instant love affair with their new wood-fired oven.

by Alan T Gray
TRENTHAM, VICTORIA

Uncles, aunties and grannies prepare their own pizzas.

IT'S HARD to convey the mix of trepidation and excitement I felt when we invited the entire family over for wood-fired pizzas on Boxing Day — for the first real test of our brand-new cob oven. I'd helped build the oven at an Alan Watt workshop (see page 32) and was very excited to get it home and put it through its paces. But would I botch it all and end up with burnt offerings instead of altar pieces?

It turned out to be a wonderful day and every pizza was cooked to perfection. We have our own system for making pizzas now: everyone has to build their own masterpiece from the toppings laid out on a nearby table. At first, some of the punters grumbled: "But I'm tired from all the Christmas rush — can't someone just Make Me A Pizza?"

But once they saw one uncle twirling his dough, granny pressing hers neatly onto the pizza tray, and three-year-old Adelaide sprinkling cheese on her Margarita, they all started to pitch in. In fact, building your own pizza from scratch is reminiscent of play dough sessions at kindergarten. It also means a little less work for the hosts. Besides, when have you EVER had a bought pizza built exactly to your mind's specifications?

Trays and peels
Alan Watt gave us great advice on where to buy pizza-making accessories. We trooped down to ABP, in Plenty Road Preston, had a ball and came home with 12 X 25 cm (ten inch) pizza trays (about $4 each).

Dough
Because I'm new to this wood-fired pizza game, I haven't yet absorbed the finer points of dough-making. At the moment pizza dough is simple: 2 kg of plain flour, 8 teaspoons of dried yeast, a pinch of salt, a gloop of top quality olive oil, all mixed together with slightly warm water and left to rise in a warm place covered with a tea towel, for a minimum of half an hour.

We have found that the dough is then best divided into individual pizza balls (bigger than a tennis ball, smaller than a lawn bowl for each 25 cm pizza — smaller or large depending on how thick you like your crust). It must then be well 'floured'. If not, then even if you 'paint' your pizza tray well with olive oil (as you must!) your pizza may still stick to the tray if the dough is damp.

If you spread your well-floured ball of pizza dough evenly onto your well-oiled tray, the half-cooked pizza will

Three-year-old Adelaide Gray adds a finishing coat of clay with a touch of Bondcrete added.

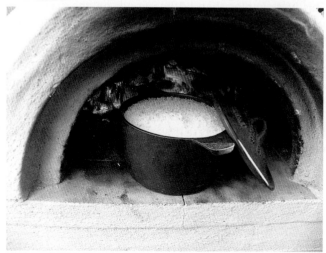
A pot of fluffy Basmati rice cooked to perfection.

slip sweetly off the tray and onto the floor of your oven when the time comes to 'brown' the bottom to a perfect "ooh-aagh" consistency.

And this is exactly what we got: heaps of groans of culinary ecstasy as people received their pizza on a wooden board, cut it themselves and tucked in.

Another tip we learned from Alan Watt we impress upon every pizza maker: do not let tomato paste and/or cheese slop onto the edge of your pizza tray! They form a food glue that makes tray removal a nightmare.

My next refinement will be to buy or scrounge a large sheet of pine plywood so I can use a jigsaw and cut out wooden 'paddles' (like a big table tennis bat) slightly larger than a pizza. You can use these paddles to replace the pizza trays entirely: use a sprinkling of polenta instead of olive oil on the bottom of

Harry Gray wields the peel on his nicely-browned garlic naan bread.

your pizza to make it slide smoothly onto the oven floor. Then once your pizza is cooked, slide it back onto the paddle: use your cutting wheel and then your paddle also becomes your plate. You can buy these pizza paddles in kitchen shops but they can cost up to $25 each: the price of an entire 2.4 m sheet of pine plywood.

Cooking in the oven

Alan Watt's cob ovens have a chimney, so there's no need to remove the fire before you start cooking. I was amazed and delighted at how little firewood we needed to cook up a storm for 15 people. Ideally, we light the oven two hours before we want to cook, but we've sometimes managed to get away with only 90 minutes of firing before cooking.

After lighting the fire with kindling, we add pieces no thicker than my thumb until the fire is roaring along and we add a few pieces about 5 cm (2 inches) square. We use plantation-grown sugar gum (*Eucalyptus cladocalyx*), which burns as hot as red gum but with far less ash — the most amazing firewood I've ever used.

When the kindling is well alight, we put the door back on the oven and only open it to add the odd piece of firewood. When the oven's been going for 90 minutes or so, we push the fire to the back of the oven, and leave the door off while we're cooking pizzas.

Judith's secret weapon

Instead of using a brass brush and 'scuffle' to clean your hot oven floor after you've pushed your fire back, we just use a coconut fibre, wooden-handles hearth brush — it works well. Once you've put a couple of pizzas in turn them after a few minutes so the edge closest to the fire doesn't burn. Then, remove the pizza tray.

It seems to be much easier to remove the pizza trays if your pizza dough has risen and the pizza is at least half-cooked. If you try to remove the pizza tray when the dough is still sloppy, you're asking for trouble.

We tend to start cooking with the temperature around 350°C, and pizzas will cook quite happily as this temperature drops as low as 100°C. If we're still cooking by then, we just throw a few thumb-width pieces of firewood into the back of the oven, and the temperature climbs back up to about 250°C in no time. We bought our temperature gauge — on a 15 cm (6 inch) stalk — for $75 at VIP Catering in Preston, Melbourne.

Harry's Indian feast

A few weeks ago, our 14-year-old son, Harry, mixed the spices to make a delicious vegetable curry, and we put one cup of rice and three cups of cold water in our trusty cast iron damper pot. We've used this cast iron mini camp oven for many years to bake fruit damper buried in outback sand. It also works perfectly for cooking rice. It took only about 12 minutes till the entire pot of rice was fluffy and perfect, and then Harry baked naan bread on the floor of the oven. As he removed the each naan we 'painted' it with garlic butter and enjoyed a delicious feast. Judith then used the cooling oven to make a superb baked custard.

Our cob oven is a delight and a hands-on fun activity for all the family. We can highly recommend one for any back yard.

•*For more details about Alan Watt's oven building workshops, held regularly throughout southern Australia, visit Alan's website at: www.woodfiredovenworkshops. com, email: woodfiredovenworkshops@bigpond.com or phone Alan on (02) 6494 0015.*

Steps to Cob Oven Heaven

Chris's oven sits on timber beams, leaving plenty of storage space beneath.

In warm weather a backyard cob oven makes perfect sense — apart from being fun to build and producing delicious food. It can even have romantic advantages, as Chris discovered. She went on to help three friends build backyard ovens and hasn't used her electric one since.

by Chris Newton

BRISBANE, QUEENSLAND

MY INSPIRATION to build a wood fire oven came from three main sources: Colin, a friend who talked endlessly about a mudbrick house his family was building, an article in *Earth Garden*, and a backyard full of highly plastic clay. I believed that I had finally found a use for that clay. Now, four years down the line we have a wood-fired oven that far exceeded my expectations, the highly plastic clay was not ideal for the job, and I have married Colin.

Design phase

Before starting to build our oven I did my time at the State Library: I needed to understand why and how to put chimneys, oven doors and vents into the plan. I discovered the basics of wood fire ovens:

1. There is no chimney. A chimney would act as a path for rising heat to escape.

2. There are no doors on the oven. The doorway is how the oven breathes. Cool air will be drawn in at the floor of the oven, provide air for the fire, and the hot air (along with any smoke when you are starting the oven) will rise to the ceiling of the oven and come out at the top of the oven doorway.

3. The height of the centre of the oven should not be greater than 350 mm. A higher ceiling will encourage the pooling of heat in this area instead of the floor of the oven where the food is cooked.

4. The doorway should be two-thirds the height of the ceiling. This encourages the storage of heat within the oven. We never had any difficulty with the oven breathing.

5. The door should be wide enough for your widest cooking dish and your hands on either side. Our doorway was 400 mm wide, though we would go wider next time so that we could put two small pizza trays in next to each other.

6. The height of the oven floor above ground is working height. I would suggest slightly higher than bench height.

7. The internal size of the oven: ours was 1200 mm round. This gave us plenty of room at the back to push the coals, leaving room at the front to cook.

The building phase

With my head around these design concepts I was next faced with the challenge of structural engineering and basic building concepts. Armed with the vision of what I wanted, and no building background, my first structure failed. At this point Colin stepped in and got my plans back on track. No wonder I married him. Here are the seven steps up to cob oven heaven.

Building sequence

1. Build your structure up to floor level. Underneath becomes a great storage area for timber. An opening here — as wide as the oven — would make for easy access. I used cob for this: a mixture of clay, straw and some manure. This was not ideal for our project. The clay was too elastic, and combined with the unprotected external environment, rain and high temperatures from the oven, it seemed doomed to crack from the early days. So we fixed it. We wrapped the oven in bird wire (for reinforcement) and gave it a cement render raincoat. It looks great and works perfectly. Use whatever suits you aesthetically: recycled bricks, Besser blocks, or maybe you would have better luck with mudbricks.

2. The floor. We placed some beams across the base and sat some secondhand corrugated iron on this. We then spread a gravel bed over the corrugated iron. We now had a floor to work from.

3. The floor and walls of the oven were made from firebricks. We got seconds. They are made for the job with excellent heat-retaining properties. Conventional bricks can be used successfully, though they may not hold the heat as long. The bricks on the floor were sat together like pavers. The bricks in the wall were two courses high and stacked in staggered fashion on top of each other.

4. The roof was also made using firebricks. Because the roof was designed as a slight dome we made some framework to support it and the doorway during construction. We used some thin ply for the framing. This was cut into wedges, like a pie, and used as a temporary ceiling. We used spare bricks, and timber struts inside the oven to support the ply framing during construction.

5. The firebricks were placed on top of the ply, radiating from the centre out to the edge. There were quite a few gaps as we radiated out. We later filled these with concrete (or Firecrete if your budget goes that far). But first we used a 12 mm threaded booker rod to run around the full circumference of the roof outer edge. We welded the ends together. This stops the roof wanting to spread and cave in once the temporary support is removed.

6. So with the roof in place with the booker rod around the edge, the gaps in the ceiling were filled with concrete and allowed to set. The spare bricks

Who wouldn't be happy with results like this?

supporting the roof were easy to remove. The ply and timber struts were burnt out on the first lighting of the oven.

7. Finish the oven as it suits you. We have three friends whose finishes are as varied as their personalities. One has chosen bricks to blend in with a suburban house, one has concrete render to blend with the rockery next to a pool, and the third has an earth render.

Getting the fire going

A fire needs lots of oxygen to get established. Light the fire in the mouth of the oven. Once it is well established, push the fire back into the oven. It will take you a bit of time to become competent at reading the oven's temperature but with a little practice you will know your oven's temperatures as well as you know your bath water temperature. Invest in a set of welding gloves because this makes turning the dishes somewhat safer: I melted the nylon kitchen mitts on the first night!

Cooking and the good life

You will be limited in your cooking possibilities only by your imagination. Get to know your oven. Experiment. This oven will make your cooking famous, because the food doesn't taste like it's from a conventional oven. Use the oven floor instead of tins to finish cooking your breads and pizza. We bake breads, pizza, biscuits, curries, casseroles, roast, whole snapper, and when the oven becomes cooler at the end of the night we use it to dry foods, and slowly cook the porridge so it is ready for breakfast.

We've had many a quiet dinner for two and quite a few parties. Friends turn up from everywhere with pizza toppings when they hear that the oven is on. It makes short work of putting on 25 pizzas for Saturday night. It's now been several years since we have used our conventional oven — we can't think of a good enough reason to use it anymore.

The Dragon's Lair

This mud oven has no cement and no flue, and not only bakes well, but it looks good too.

by Bruce Hedge
NEWHAM, VICTORIA

SEAN and Peter own Hesket House, a beautiful owner-built secluded reception centre tucked away in the forest near Romsey in central Victoria. As their catering needs expanded, the idea of an outdoor oven to cook pizzas and canapés, and bake bread as a supplement to their main meals, became more attractive. They chose a spectacular site for their oven, overlooking the lake, surrounded by herbs and flowers, and set to researching all the different styles of traditional ovens from around the world.

"I googled 'mudbrick ovens' on the internet and got over thirty thousand sites", Peter told me, "and we settled on a style without a chimney made from three external layers, which we've christened our 'Dragon's Lair'".

Construction started after filling a rock base with granitic sand, and very carefully levelling and compacting the site. They planned to use no cement at all in the construction, after reading numerous reports of cracking in existing ovens that used cement. A base of tightly packed smooth fire bricks was laid. They took particular care to ensure the base was completely smooth and level so that tools and implements like pizza slides didn't get caught as they were being removed. It was also important to be dead level for evenness of temperature across the whole base during cooking. Then the fun started.

Forming the dome
A rather large sand dome was constructed from brickies' sand about a metre in diameter and about eighty centimetres high. The sand dome was smoothed to become the mould over which the oven was constructed. The critical aspect of this chimney-less design is the height of the door, and most designs suggested a figure of about 65 per cent of the internal height. The door

opening was fashioned after the internal cob mix was in place. Peter says that an oven like this has to breathe. The mixture for the inside of the oven is a very slightly moist pisé-like mix of granitic sand and good clay.

The ingredients were trampled in heavy builder's plastic until uniform, then jumped on and flattened into a slab from which bricks about 15 cm by 10 cm by 5 cm were cut to make the first layer. These bricks spiralled around the perimeter up to the peak as shown in the photo. The door was cut and the edges finished, making sure it was wide enough to accommodate a pizza tray. The Lair's door was made from seasoned redgum to fit the hole snugly.

The next layer is an insulation layer consisting of a mixture of straw and perlite, a few centimetres thick. The final external layer is a waterproofing cover made from a mix of fresh cow manure and clay five centimetres thick. Then came the decorative touches to complement the Dragon's Lair. That's a clay tree trunk growing on top of the Lair, not a chimney!!

Test drive
After about a week of drying and curing came the big moment: the first firing.

A gentle fire was started on one side and Peter and Sean watched with trepidation as the Lair slowly heated up and steamed in the cool air. Their research had paid off, as the fire drew air in from the outside and burned smoothly and evenly as fuel was added. The steaming stopped after a while, and only a few minor small cracks appeared on the surface — a normal occurrence if granitic sand is used. These cracks are easily filled, and the oven had passed its first firing with flying colours.

Peter and Sean have learned to drive their oven depending on what they are cooking. For pizzas, a three to four hour firing is necessary to get the heat up. Peter says that the right temperature for pizzas is when you can hold your bare hand at the doorway for

Sean and Peter's Pizza Beer Dough

2–3 cups plain flour

1 stubby Coopers ale or other beer

1 pinch salt

Dash olive oil

Mix to a dryish dough, and let it rest for an hour before use.

Smoothing the sand mould on a level base.

Looking as if it had grown there, the oven has been a winner.

seven seconds. The fire can be left in for pizzas, but for roasts and bread, the coals are raked out, and the door put in place.

In retrospect, they would have made two modifications. Firstly, the base would be insulated underneath from the surrounding rocks and earth by a similar insulation layer as in the oven's walls. Secondly, the inside of the oven would have been roughened to improve thermal retention. Something to do with surface area, they suspect.

In all, it was a wonderful productive exercise that has proved extremely useful in their business, and has proved a great talking point. Every home should have one!

An Oven Named Yuri

by Angela Rockel

GLAZIERS BAY, TASMANIA

I BUILT Yuri using a framework of willow sticks from the hedge nearby with a thick layer of newspaper over the top, followed by mud from the excavation we made for a building project. The soil here is good for mudbricks — enough sand to stop the clay cracking. I put on a layer of mud about 3 cm thick each day for four days to make the dome, with an old enamel basin propped in place as a form for the oven opening. Of course once the dome was in place it was clear that it wanted eyes and then one thing led to another: nose, ears (one of which became a smoke-hole), haunches, front paws, tail . . .

I kept the whole thing damp and covered for a couple of weeks to cure before lighting a small fire.

He loves to cook with yeast — pizza, bread, strudel — and also bakes a mean spud. Yuri is very economical fuel-wise and works best burning twiggy sticks rather than split wood: I'm cleaning up under the windbreaks.

All those folktales populated by people out gathering bundles of faggots start to make sense: one bundle and an hour from lighting and he's ready to rock. I'm sorry I was too impatient to make a proper floor of bricks — he's just sitting on the ground and that makes for an uneven cooking surface and probably means he won't weather very well. At the moment I just put a plastic sheet over the top when it rains.

Above: the cuddly Yuri oven.

Right: Yuri cooks dinner, with Sue Moss (l) and Angela Rockel (r).

Below: yummy Yuri food.

All photographs by Julie Hunt.

Chapter Two

Brick, Stone & Cement

Ancient Form for Backyard Oven

by Margaret and John Tasey

MINTO HEIGHTS,
NEW SOUTH WALES

I T WAS a great backyard project with many problems to solve. Our inspiration came from the Trulli houses of Puglia, the great work on catenary arches and vaults at Auroville, India, and thirdly, Rado's enthusiastic website www.traditionaloven. com.au.

There's something about the size of an oven that makes it a wonderful building project.

We've had some great meals from the oven, and last weekend served roast beef to 30 people for my mother's 95th birthday.

1. We started with a piece of old storm-water pipe dropped onto our foundation slab (inset).

2. We employed a bricklayer to build the refractory part of the oven on the second slab to our specifications (above right).

3. It was then clad with a layer of commons and concrete to make the walls 225 mm (9 inches) thick. Some lovely old bricks and blocks made the tunnel and chimney (right).

4. Using the principle of the catenary arch, John built a separate Hebel dome not touching the oven. We filled this space with vermiculite (above left).

5. Then we rendered it with high performance concrete (above right).

6. And waterproofed it — probably completely unnecessary. Then we wrapped the whole thing in stone (left).

RECIPE

Apples Baked in Sour Cream Pudding

In a large shallow ceramic dish mix together

60 g soft butter

3/4 cup plain flour

1 1/2 tsp baking pdr

1/2 tsp vanilla

1/4 tsp salt

1/2 cup sugar

1/3 cup milk

Add one egg and mix

Sprinkle with 1 cup packed brown sugar

Pour over 1 cup sour cream

Take 6 or 7 small Granny Smith apples, core them and peel the bottom half and set into the pudding. Stuff with caramelised prunes and bake in a slow oven for about an hour.

Our first homemade pizza.

The completed dome. It is so well insulated it stays hot for days.

Alan and Odette's oven has pride of place in the garden.

The Rose Garden Oven

by Bruce Hedge
NEWHAM, VICTORIA

THIS oven was hard physical work! After doing a one-day course on building ovens, Alan Hebb and Odette Spruyt selected the site for their showstopper. Or rather, the site selected itself in their beautiful rose-filled garden. The design called for a base with a wood storage area. An archway was built of timber, and bricks were laid up and over the frame, with conventional mortar to keep them in place. The base of the oven was then constructed, and allowed to set for a few weeks.

The project took almost eight months off and on, and varies from others in that it has a chimney hole above the door. No insulation was used, the oven's walls being a uniform mix of bricks and clay. The finishing touches were pieces of slate left over from other jobs, and a sliding door made of timber, with metal beaten around the timber to fit the hole. The wooden part burnt away fairly quickly, however, leaving the metal fitting snugly as the door. The door can slide in to close the oven off to retain heat for bread and roasts, but sliding it out exposes the chimney and lets the fire inside burn.

Alan found that a hole about 15 cm by 5 cm at the bottom of the door was necessary to allow the fire to draw properly. A slow initial firing took place, but now the oven is used to cook great pizzas and entertain friends. Alan and Odette's favourite pizza topping is thin slices of cooked potato drizzled with a marinade of olive oil infused with rosemary and garlic, with capers and/or anchovies.

Community Wood-fired Ovens

Building a wood-fired oven is a great community project with a tasty result at the end of the work. Here Amadis describes two Melbourne ones.

by Amadis Lacheta

COBURG NORTH, VICTORIA

Tony and Minh at work on the base of the Braybrook oven.

BOTH the wood-fired oven at the Garden of Eden in Albert Park and the Braybrook Community Garden in Melbourne were inspired by Alan Scott of Ovencrafters in Petaluma, CA, USA. I have also come across a couple more wood-fired ovens that were inspired by Ovencrafters, namely the bakery oven at Crystal Waters Permaculture Village in the Sunshine Coast hinterland, and the bakery oven at CERES in Brunswick, Melbourne, where Ken sells a variety of artisan breads at the Saturday morning market. I wouldn't be surprised if there were many more, and I think it's worth sharing a little history with you.

Ovencrafters began as a request from Laurel Robertson, who is a friend and also the author of *Laurel's Kitchen Bread Book*. She asked me to build a brick oven for her kitchen. When the first loaves emerged from that oven I knew that something lost was miraculously being rebirthed. Since this beginning in 1982 many other long lost aspects of bread baking, milling and growing grains have been rediscovered; even wood heat has revealed itself to be the only ecologically sound, sustainable and non-polluting source of energy for small scale bakeries. However it is largely the inimitable deep penetrating heat of the masonry ovens that has triggered much of this work.

Ovencrafters' purpose is to earn a right livelihood for its staff guided by Gandhian principles, particularly: "Policy with principles, commerce with morality, wealth through work, and science with humanity". Ovencrafters' oven designs and self building processes are inspiring a return to nourishing, handmade bread in the family home, and at a local level. — From http://www.ovencrafters.net.

Construction

Both the Garden of Eden and Braybrook ovens were created from Alan Scott's DIY plans, and constructed by participants of Work for the Dole programs coordinated by the Garden

Two ovens, one design. The Braybrook oven (left) and the Garden of Eden oven (far left) show some of the variations that are possible.

of Eden under the supervision of landscaper Tony Cudmore. I myself did a crash course in this form of oven building, deciphering sometimes quixotic plans while endeavouring to lead our ever-willing volunteers at the Braybrook Community Garden. Once you get the hang of it, and provided you get the size of the oven dimensions right in relation to the door size, it's relatively straightforward. The ovens are built from a Hebel brick base, with cast iron frame for the upper oven, fire bricks for the hearth, and just recycled house bricks for the arch of the oven. This is then rendered and insulated with a mixture of vermiculite and cement, and decorated with any flair and imagination you can muster. For added colour, you can mix an oxide in the render. The chimney can be constructed from metal or heavy ceramic, and the door from recycled wood, with an insulated layer in between the wood exterior, and metal interior. A few handy folk and the right tools will be all you need.

These ovens have given birth to many tasty pizzas, loaves of bread and delicious baked vegetables, cooked by friends, children, Work for the Dole participants and volunteers. Of course, the beauty of this kind of baking is that you can cook a number of different dishes, commencing with those that require fast cooking and a high heat, to those that can be baked slowly at lower temperatures as the oven cools down. With both of these ovens, a fire is created within the baking chamber until the heat required is achieved, and then the coals are removed to leave space for the food itself. This means a significant thermal mass is needed for the baking chamber to store and release the heat over time.

Pizza Margherita

Simple and delicious. I am so enamoured of pizza that I created a pizza-shaped vegetable patch (six slices) in our front yard, which naturally grows what you would find on top of pizzas: tomatoes, capsicum, basil, chillies and eggplant. This recipe is based on one from a wonderful book called *The Food of Italy*. The classic Margherita Pizza was supposedly invented in 1889 by Raffaele Esposito in honour of Queen Margherita. The Queen had heard so much of the fabled pizzas of Naples that she requested one to eat when she visited the city.

RECIPE

Pizza Margherita

Base

(makes 2 x 30 cm pizza bases)

1 tblsp caster sugar

2 tsp dried yeast or 15 g fresh yeast

215 ml lukewarm water

450 g plain flour

1/2 tsp salt

3 tbsp olive oil

1 tbsp cornmeal

Put the sugar and yeast in a small bowl and stir in 90 ml of the water. Leave in a draught-free, warm spot to activate. Mix the flour and salt in a bowl, add the olive oil, remaining water and the yeast mixture. Mix until the dough loosely clumps together. Transfer to a lightly floured surface and knead until you have a soft dough that is not sticky but dry to the touch. Add a little flour or a few drops of warm water if needed. Rub the inside of a large bowl with olive oil. Roll the ball of dough around in the bowl to coat it with oil.

Cover the bowl with a tea towel, pop back in your draught-free warm spot, and leave for one and a half hours or until doubled in size. Remove the dough and punch down to its original size. Split into two portions, and working with one at a time use the heel of your hands to create the base. Place on a lightly oiled tray dusted with the cornmeal, ready for your favourite toppings.

Topping

6 medium-sized home-grown tomatoes (or 1 tin of organic peeled tomatoes)

1 tsp sugar

1/2 tsp salt

Pepper to taste

A handful of thyme

1 large clove of garlic

2 tsp olive oil

A handful of fresh basil leaves

150 g mozzarella, thinly sliced

In a small pan, heat the oil and fry the crushed garlic, making sure the garlic does not burn. Add the thyme and chopped tomatoes, sugar, salt and pepper. Allow the tomato sauce to reduce on low heat for 10 minutes or so. Spread the tomato sauce on the pizza bases, and scatter the mozzarella and basil leaves, drizzling the pizza with a little olive oil. Bake in a hot wood-fired oven (240°C if you have a thermometer) for 12–15 minutes until crisp and golden.

The meeting place is designed as a seed pod with the oven as the seed.

Duck Flat Community Garden
Seed Pod Oven

Originating as a functional sculpture project, this flueless masonry oven and its setting are just the thing for tasty and sociable community activities.

by Chris Banks
NAIRNE, SOUTH AUSTRALIA

THE PLANTING of food, its tending, picking and eating, is such a pleasurable activity made all the more sociable by cooking it in a community garden wood-fired pizza oven.

Our garden was fortunate to be the venue for a visual arts student who wanted to create a piece of functional sculpture for one of her projects. She designed a meeting place in the shape of a seed pod which was the seating and the oven at the centre was the seed.

The plinth is made from recycled bricks and filled with rubble so it stands waist high with two recesses to store firewood. The dome was made from old half bricks shaped to form a circle and with each course mud was packed in to tilt the outer edge to form the dome. As the curve comes in it is wise to pack the dome with straw or shredded paper to hold the shape. For the last part, the circle of bricks must be carefully shaped so they lock together with their own weight. At this stage an extra pair of hands is essential so it doesn't collapse. Since we don't have a chimney at the front, the hole at the top has a carefully shaped bung, which is removed to light the fire. Once it is going with coals the bung is replaced to keep the heat inside.

We've had many successful gatherings with people of all ages and abilities preparing food, cooking and enjoying the ambience. It's a great way to entertain a large group because the preparation can be shared and it doesn't all have to be ready at the same time. It pays to have a few people who know how to get the temperature right and that depends on wood quality, timing and the season of the year.

Roasted vegetables of any sort are delicious with or without pizza but don't put the oil in the pan — rub the vegetables in it and turn occasionally. We cooked our homegrown pumpkins in two minutes with a flash of light and they were so black you couldn't eat them!

The bricks must lock together under their own weight. Extra hands are essential.

Above: many have cooked and eaten and enjoyed the experience here. The bung is visible at the top. (Photo by Richard Telford.)

Paved floor completed, rendering almost done.

Red Beard Bakery

Does a bakery with an oven the size of two VWs need a backyard oven? Al and John decided it did, and dug into oven history to design one that would bake good bread.

by Al and John Reid

TRENTHAM, VICTORIA

It's all about thermal mass

You might wonder why, with our huge and beautiful 120-year-old wood-fired Scotch oven, we at Red Beard Bakery would want to build a backyard oven. Well, it seems that people just can't get enough good wood-fired food.

When we started our business 18 months ago we never imagined that we would run out of capacity in our Scotch oven, which is big enough to garage two VW Beetles (13 square metres), if you could squeeze

them through the small oven door! However, with business booming and the introduction of pizza nights on Saturdays, we no longer had room in our baking schedule for both sourdough bread and pizzas.

We decided to build an Alan Scott-style Roman masonry oven in our café courtyard. Now our customers can watch one of our bakers creating and baking the pizzas in our new oven outside, while the rest of our team produces the bread uninterrupted in the Scotch oven inside the bakery.

John Reid first experienced an Alan Scott oven at the wonderful Fruition Bakery near Healesville, Victoria, run by his friend and fellow sourdough baker Ian Banfield. John was impressed with the oven's heat retention and the high quality bread it delivered. He subsequently attended one of Alan Scott's oven building workshops and was even more impressed with the ease of construction and use of readily-available materials. John has also built a couple of other styles of backyard oven, including a cob oven at the CERES Environment Park in Melbourne.

Masonry and cob ovens

Roman masonry ovens and cob (aka adobe) ovens work in quite different ways. While this may be explained elsewhere in this book, it's a point worth reiterating. Roman ovens, like Scotch ovens, work by storing heat in their massive masonry structures — called thermal mass — which is released gradually and smoothly. A typical backyard Roman oven, such as those Alan Scott has helped people to build for 25 years (see www.ovencrafters.net), will contain at least two tonnes of thermal mass.

Due to their thermal mass, the fire in Roman ovens can be removed completely before baking commences, so that the bread or pizza is bathed in deep and even heat rather than searing heat from burning coals. This technological advance occurred in Roman times, and was a big improvement on cob ovens.

Roman ovens, like Scotch ovens, work by storing heat in their massive masonry structures — called thermal mass — which is released gradually and smoothly. A typical backyard Roman oven, such as those Alan Scott has helped people to build for 25 years, will contain at least two tonnes of thermal mass.

Cob ovens, which are still used extensively in Asia and the Middle East, are cheaper and easier to build and represent the earliest oven technology. They are generally made from a local clay and a plant fibre mixture, which can be shaped into beautiful organic designs. By comparison we had to work hard to make our Roman oven look good!

Just as in mudbrick and strawbale houses, clay is better at insulating than storing heat. Cob ovens

rely largely on heat radiating directly from the fire itself rather than from the oven structure to cook the dough. Unfortunately this makes the baking process harder to control and often leads to charred bread and pizzas.

Scotch ovens

While Alan Scott has created possibly the only backyard oven that bakes bread well, he admits that it does not approach the perfection of a commercial Scotch oven. The advent of Scotch, Vienna, and other side-flued masonry ovens 250 years ago represented a huge advance on Roman ovens. The fire was removed from the floor of the oven and placed over a grate where air can easily pass through it, creating a furnace effect — the timber burns more efficiently, the heat is distributed more evenly, and the floor does not have to be cleared of coals before baking.

The internal layer of bricks is encased in a bed of sand and the whole oven is tied together with steel rods top and bottom, allowing the oven to contract and expand without pulling itself apart. While our Scotch oven has almost no cracks after 120 years, major fault lines can appear in backyard ovens after the first firing. An average backyard oven may bake eight or nine loaves per firing, whereas Red Beard Bakery's Scotch oven regularly bakes one hundred times as many loaves per firing.

Most good modern bakeries now use electric/gas multi-level deck ovens. In recent times they have tried to recapture the benefits of thermal mass by reintroducing fire bricks on the floor of each level, but the bread produced is still inferior. Our preliminary calculations also suggest that the fuel cost and greenhouse emissions of a Scotch oven are much lower than for a deck oven with similar capacity.

A final word of advice for backyard oven builders regarding thermal mass: the more the merrier. We had to wait two weeks after firing our Scotch oven to crawl inside and do some minor repairs on the firebox, and it was still holding 57°C with all the doors open. Seventy five tonnes of thermal mass takes quite a while to cool down.

Thaïs Sansom and John Reid from Red Beard Bakery with their newly-built masonry oven. Red Beard Bakery was recently described by 'The Age' newspaper's 'Foodie's Guide To Melbourne' as: " . . . probably country Victoria's best new food store". Visit redbeardbakery.com.au for details.

The All Night Brick Oven

This masonry oven lives indoors, so it needs a flue. Tibor took lessons from a local man with the necessary experience, and in a short space of time the oven was turning out mouthwatering dishes, for which Aggie shares some of her secrets.

by Tibor and Aggie Kassay

LANGWARRIN, VICTORIA

BOTH myself and my wife Aggie had admired brick ovens for many years and looked through books and the internet for ideas. Of course, not being a bricklayer, I decided to do a basic course in brick oven making with a local Greek guy in his back yard. Once I was armed with the necessary information, I set out to design our oven and accumulate our leftover bricks from when we built the house (fire bricks were not needed).

I started with a concrete slab, on which I built the base and filled it with rubble onto which I laid another slab inside the base. On this slab I laid a layer of bricks on a bed of sand, which became the floor of the oven. Marking out the oval shape (and making a ply template) I started laying bricks with smooth sides inside. The dome was built up and supported by lengths of scrap timber.

When the dome was finished I covered it in a mixture of clay and straw, about 25 mm thick, then applied 100 mm of insulation batts covered in chicken wire and finished with a 25 to 50 mm layer of mortar (which condensed the batts).

When cured and fired for the first time it was as solid as a brick outhouse!

A flue is used in our situation as it is under cover. We used stainless steel so it would not rust.

All up it took approximately two to three weeks (part time) allowing for drying time.

Cooking in our Brick Oven

It was all trial and error at first, but after a few burnt offerings we have mastered the art of cooking in our brick oven!

We fire it up for approximately three to four hours. Why so long? To get the heat deep into the bricks. Once it is fired up, and the coals have burnt down, remove the coals (as you are cooking with radiant heat) and you are now ready to cook.

As the oven is really hot at this stage, you can start with cooking pizzas for lunch, throw a roast and/or lasagne in for dinner (you can also bake your bread at this stage), or if you prefer a European-style crusty loaf of bread, wait until the roast is finished (as the temperature is lower and it takes longer for your bread to cook, you achieve that lovely thick crust). YUM!

Your brick oven is still lovely and warm and (if fired correctly) it will stay that way right through the night. So, at this stage, you can put together your favourite stew/casserole makings and place into the oven. Close the door and leave overnight. The next morning — hey presto, you have another great meal already prepared for dinner. All from the one firing. ENJOY !

Building the dome, with chip wedges and sticks for support.

Tibor fired up and ready to go after a job well done.

RECIPES

Aggie's Garden Fresh Pizza

Use your favourite bread dough for base, and enough ingredients to suit number and size of pizzas you would like.

1 ripe tomato (or halve and place under griller)
Red capsicum (thinly sliced)
Extra tomatoes
Thyme leaves
Baby spinach (washed)
Sliced cooked pumpkin
Ricotta or feta cheese
Anchovies (optional)
Fresh basil leaves (chopped)
Sliced black or green olives (optional)

Lightly grease pizza tray with olive oil, pat bread dough into tray and brush lightly with olive oil. Slice one tomato in half and smear onto dough then thinly slice remaining tomatoes and place on top. Next, top with baby spinach leaves and layer all other ingredients as you please. Finish with fresh basil and thyme leaves.

Cook in hot brick oven for approximately 10 to 15 minutes.

Aggie's Vegie Lasagne

Lasagne sheets
2 eggs, beaten
3 cloves garlic/fresh basil leaves
1 tsp mixed spice
6 silver beet leaves
2 cups cooked pumpkin, mashed
2 cups ricotta cheese
Shredded tasty cheese
4 ripe tomatoes roughly diced
1 large onion
Salt & pepper
3 rashers lean bacon (optional)
Grated tasty cheese
Salad makings

Cook onion in olive oil until transparent, add crushed garlic, tomatoes, chopped basil leaves, spice, salt and pepper. Mix until heated through. Let simmer while you wash and chop silver beet. If using bacon, chop and cook lightly in deep frypan or wok, add silver beet and cook until leaves reduce in size. Add ricotta cheese and mix well. Have cooked (mashed) pumpkin ready.

In a large oiled casserole dish, place a third of the lasagne sheets, then layer with tomato sauce, pumpkin, silver beet mix, eggs and tasty cheese. Start over in that order and continue until all ingredients used.

Top with more tasty cheese, salt and pepper and cook in wood oven for approximately 40 minutes until brown on top.

Serve with tossed salad of your choice.

Wood-fired Oven at Ellender Estate

A wide variety of great food can come from a masonry oven. Read what Graham and Jenny have to say. You may be surprised.

by Graham and Jenny Ellender

GLENLYON, VICTORIA

ANCIENT Romans celebrated the seventeenth of February each year with the 'Festa Fornicalia' when the Goddess of Ovens — Fornax — was worshipped. The oven in Roman Days represented the creation of life and has in time given rise to the expression 'bun in the oven' and the verb *to fornicate*!

The wood-fired oven still represents creation — especially artistic re-creation of traditional and rustic foods. Once food from a wood-fired oven is savoured another dimension is experienced.

At Ellender Estate, an Alan Scott oven has been built and is fired up each week for guests of Ellender Estate Winery. Routinely, breads — whole grain and lees breads — are baked and then the fire relit for a selection of pizzas: Istra prosciutto and salami, vegetarian, Tuki trout or Tallegio and mushroom. Later in the day the oven is used for the family weekly roast. Rib eye beef, lamb, chicken, rabbit, venison and pork with roast vegetables have all been cooked with great success. Vegetables such as whole-roasted baby beetroots, carrots, pumpkin, Jerusalem artichokes, onions and potatoes mixed with garlic and fresh thyme leaves, salt and pepper and Kyneton Olive Oil are favourites for large functions.

Special events during the Central Victorian Slow Food Convivium at Ellender Estate, with guest chef Maria Pia from Wellington, New Zealand, featured goat cooked in the oven. Maria, originally from Italy, decorated the oven with mimosa (wattle) to remind her of her homeland, Puglia. Hands-on bread making and oven building workshops are featured throughout the year.

In 2006 at the annual Macedon Ranges Wine Region Budburst Festival event at Ellender Estate, 'Porchetta' Suckling Pig was served in the traditional Italian manner with bread baked from the wood-fired oven, served with Country Cuisine Onion and Cranberry Chutney. The suckling pig, boned, seasoned with fresh herbs and rolled, was cooked for five hours in the oven.

The tradition of villagers cooking their casseroles in the wood-fired oven after the baker has finished the daily baking, was experienced by Daylesford and Glenlyon locals who brought their casseroles to cook in the oven and share — a great local event. Blueberries from the Glenlyon Nutty Fruit Farm appeared for dessert and a quick Clafoutis was whipped up, blueberries added, and cooked in a small round pan in the oven — delicious with cream. Don't be scared to experiment — it is what a wood-fired oven is all about!

Although fired each week the oven remains hot for several days and warm until refired the next weekend, lending itself later in the week to oven-dried tomatoes and eventually meringues.

The style of our oven enables a large store of heat which is dissipated into the chamber — the fire is removed from the chamber for bread baking, cakes, biscuits, muffins, casseroles and slow roasts, but for roasting, tandoori and pizza making the fire is left in either at the back or, in the case of tandoori, either side. All foods are moist and have a dimension not obtained in a conventional household oven.

Close proximity to the
fire gives a pizza its authentic texture and taste.
Tallegio and mushroom (left), Fromage Frais (right).

RECIPES

Tallegio and Mushroom: an Adult Pizza

Prepare pizza base to your own design and roll out a ball of dough (5 cm sphere) to 3 mm thick on a floured surface. Place on an oiled baking tray. Place slivers of Tallegio cheese dotted over the surface, and then slice mushrooms. Sprinkle with cracked pepper.

Place into the oven, which has a fire alight in the back. Cook until slight browning of the edge nearest the fire, turn round until fully cooked (you can slip the pizza off the tray onto the cleaned slab once cooking is underway).

Serve garnished with wild roquette and slices of pear.

Smoked Trout and Fromage Frais

Prepare pizza base as above and coat with a liberal layer of Holy Goat Fromage Frais. Place pieces of filleted Tuki smoked trout over the Fromage Frais and place in the oven and cook as above. Serve garnished with dill.

Wholegrain bread

2 lb wholegrain flour
1 lb plain bread flour
4 oz mixed grain
8 oz cracked malt grain
1 3/4 tsp salt
3 tbsp malted wheat flour
2 tbsp yogurt
2 tbsp plus malt extract
33 fl oz warm water
2 oz yeast
3 fl oz extra virgin olive oil

Place flours, salt and yoghurt in warm bowl and mix. Pour half the water–malt mixture over the grains and soften for 30 minutes then after fifteen minutes mix the yeast into the remaining water and allow to become active for fifteen minutes.

Mix the grain, yeast mixture, oil and knead for 5 minutes. Leave in a covered bowl for two hours in a warm spot. Knead and place in bread baking tins or trays and prove for 30 minutes in a warm and moist environment.

Place into the prepared oven with fire raked out and tempered with a mop and water to achieve a roof temperature around 220°C and floor temperature 180°C — spray a little water into the oven and seal the oven with a tight fitting door.

Bake until sounds hollow — approximately 35 to 40 minutes (depends on the temperature). Allow to cool on a baking rack.

RECIPES

Fruit Tarts

For a quick easy dessert using fruits in season, I have used white nectarines, pears and strawberries. Serve with cream.

two sheets of frozen butter puff pastry
nectarines, peaches, pears or strawberries
JC Bee Honey

Cut each sheet into six pieces and place on baking tray lined with baking paper. Slice fruit and place slices overlapping onto each piece. Drizzle with a little honey, top with oven-roasted chopped pistachio nuts and bake in the hot oven approximately 8 minutes or until golden and puffed.

For the strawberry tarts I have spread a dessertspoon of Holy Goat Fromage Frais on the pastry and topped with the sliced strawberries.

Poached Quinces

Place washed, peeled and quartered quinces in a large covered casserole dish with a sugar syrup (two parts water to one part sugar) and bake in the cooling oven for six hours.

For a quick easy dessert use puff pastry and fruits in season. Serve with cream.

• Ellender Estate is in Green Gully Road, Glenlyon, Victoria, phone (03) 5348 7785, web: www.ellenderwines.com.au.

Il Fornaio
Lavandula's
Wood Oven

Lavandula is well known for its good food and attractive surroundings. Here chef Jarrett Volke reveals some of the secrets (and recipes) behind the appetising dishes from the Lavandula oven.

by Gael Shannon and Jarratt Volke

SHEPHERDS FLAT, VICTORIA

The heart of Italian food is the heat of the wood oven.

Jarratt checking the roast. The design is based on the traditional pizza oven used to conserve firewood.

L AVANDULA grows lavender, olives and grapes around golden stone farm buildings constructed by Italians in the 1860s. A farmhouse, a barn and a small dairy cluster around a cobbled courtyard. Beyond is a garden, a creek and the rolling farm hills. It's a productive farm that looks beautiful. It feels entirely European with its tall poplars and swathes of deciduous trees, and it's also very slow food.

The slow food movement (begun in northern Italy to oppose fast foods) links food and pleasure with eco-awareness and accountability. Its members believe there's a special satisfaction that comes from taking the time to enjoy good food and drink, grown well, cooked well, and shared in good company. So at Lavandula in-season food is grown on the creek flats and harvested for use that day at La Trattoria: salad greens, herbs and vegetables, fruit, nuts and berries; from the olive grove, olive oil is pressed and other varieties are pickled. The grapes are pressed for Lavandula's own vintage. And the lavender is distilled, or dried and bagged and made into a range of fragrant body products.

The daytime café was inspired by the typical grotto of Ticino (in southern Switzerland where they speak Italian and little cafés are tucked away among the huge granite rocks or in the cool of a glade of trees). Good Italian food is of course *al forno*, straight from the wood oven. For flavour, and for volume cooking at the right temperature, Lavandula had to have a wood oven. It is used weekly to cook meats and roast

vegetables; on other special occasions it has roasted suckling pig or a flight of fowl, or at festivals, volumes of gourmet pizza.

Three years ago the oven was built by Alan Watt; fire bricks and high-temperature castable cement was bagged in an ochre to blend with the heritage sandstone farm buildings. Constructed early in Alan's oven building career, this did not contain materials that were subsequently to prove of benefit — stainless steel needles for reinforcement and a space-age ceramic blanket for excellent insulation.

The form is a modification of the typical pizza oven traditionally used by all villagers to conserve firewood. It has a chimney rising from the front of the oven allowing a broad range of cooking styles. The oven sits above a large space for storing dry firewood, and beside it is a barbecue.

Alan returned to fire up the oven for the first time to dry out all the materials and season it. He kept a low small flame (you can use coals from a fire elsewhere), and built up the heat gradually to baking temperature. One evening the oven was given its maiden baking with a variety of pizzas created by staff and friends.

RECIPES

Roasting chicken in a wood-fired oven

Ingredients

1 whole organic chicken

Sage butter:

200 g softened butter

1 tbsp chopped fresh sage

2 cloves garlic, minced

Zest of one lemon

1 tsp sea salt

1 tsp cracked black pepper

100 ml olive oil

2 lemons

Sea salt

Cracked black pepper

Procedure

Combine all ingredients for the sage butter. With a boning knife insert a slit at the bottom of the skin on the front and back of the chicken. Gently run your fingers under the skin separating it from the chicken. Rub the sage butter under the skin and stuff the chicken with remaining butter. With one whole lemon stuff the chicken.

Brush the entire surface of the chicken with olive oil and season the skin well with salt and pepper. Place in a roasting tray, cut one lemon in half and place in the tray.

Ensure your wood-fired oven is at a steady temperature between 100°C and 150°C.

Place the chicken in the oven. Turn after 20 minutes. After 40 minutes flip the chicken over. After 60 minutes turn the chicken. After 80 minutes the chicken should be cooked through and have a slightly charred appearance.

Remove the chicken from the oven, leave in the hot tray, cover with foil and allow to rest for 15 minutes.

Lighting the wood oven

Summary

The heat of the fire is absorbed by the oven walls. When the dome is white hot, let the fire die down or burn gently till you've finished cooking. Use the final heat for an overnight task. Sweep out the ash — you can keep the coals for the next fire.

Lighting the fire

Crumple some aged newspaper and top it with a good quantity of kindling (sticks). When they are burning well, put on some bigger dry branches, and once the fire is beginning to consolidate and create some coals, put on one heavier piece of firewood. Build more wood for at least an hour to reach the desired temperature. Let it build slowly so the temperature will be well absorbed and evenly distributed. The heat will be determined by the wood you use — pine and wattle are HOT. It may smoke then and be quite flame-y. NEVER use particle board or green treated pine, even scraps!!

If you want to cook pizzas, keep the wood small, perhaps just kindling, and push it to one side. Cook the pizza on the floor of the oven on the other side. It'll take two or three minutes.

If you want to cook bigger food wait till you've burned most wood and reached top temperature, push the coals aside and pop in the food. Close the oven door and wait until it's cooked. Cooking is done as the heat fades.

If you want to cook bread (slower and longer than pizzas) close the oven with a specially constructed wooden door that you can soak in water — that creates steam inside.

The oven may stay hot enough for five or six hours, so plan what else can go in there — herbs or fruit to dry.

To clean out the ash, rake it to the centre and take it out on your pizza paddle.

• Lavandula is open daily 10.30am to 5.30pm, café closed August, farm closed Christmas Eve/Christmas Day. Entry $3.50/$1. Annual membership $10.
Pets on a lead are welcome.
Ten minutes north of Daylesford, Victoria on the Hepburn–Newstead Road, Melway 609 C8 www.lavandula.com.au Ph: (03) 5476 4393.

References:
www.alforno.com.au
www.traditionaloven.com/tutorials

Lamb legs from the oven. Mmm — not bad at all.

Roasting lamb in a wood-fired oven

Ingredients

1 whole leg of lamb, bone intact.
Marinade:
Zest and juice of 2 lemons
1 tbsp of chopped fresh rosemary
2 cloves of garlic crushed
Good sea salt flakes
Fine cracked black pepper
200 ml olive oil

Procedure

Mix all the marinade ingredients together. Score the top and the bottom of the lamb. Pour the marinade over the top and underside of the lamb and massage into the meat. Then sprinkle a crust of sea salt over the whole surface. If possible the lamb should be marinaded the day before cooking.

Ensure your wood oven is at a steady temperature between 100°C and 150°C. This will ensure tenderness. Roasting at a high temperature will make your lamb tough.

Place lamb in a roasting tray and let it warm to room temperature. Then place in the oven. After twenty minutes turn the lamb. After 40 minutes flip the lamb over. After 60 minutes turn the lamb. After 80 minutes your lamb should have a slightly charred appearance, and is now ready to take out of the oven and rest. Keep the lamb on the hot tray and cover in foil for 15 to 20 minutes. Your lamb is now ready to carve.

Wood-fired pumpkin, leek and chickpea pie

Ingredients

3 butternut pumpkins
3 cups of chickpeas
3 leeks
2 cloves garlic crushed
3 eggs
2 cups fresh ricotta
2 cups olive oil
Salt and pepper to taste
Egg and milk wash — 2 cups of milk, 1 egg. Whisk together

Procedure

If your chickpeas are dried, soak them overnight before cooking them. If in brine, strain and rinse well.

Dice pumpkin into one-centimetre cubes. Spray a baking tray and place pumpkin on it. Drizzle the pumpkin with olive oil and season well with salt and pepper.

Warm the wood-fired oven to 250°C. Place the pumpkin in the oven. After five minutes turn. Repeat until the pumpkin has a charred appearance and is cooked but not mushy.

Take the pumpkin out of the oven and put to the side. Allow the oven to cool to 100°C.

While the oven is cooling, sauté off the leek and garlic in a pan. In a mixing bowl combine the leek, garlic, pumpkin, 3 eggs, chickpeas and season well.

Spray your pie dishes with canola spray. Cut out the puff pastry and line the pie dishes. Use your egg and milk wash to brush the pastry. Place on a baking tray and par-bake in the oven which should now be cooled to 100°C. When the pastry has risen but not yet coloured, take out of the oven. Fill the pastries with the pie mix, then sprinkle the tops with chunks of ricotta.

Place the pies back in the oven, turning them every five minutes. When the pie has risen a centimetre or so, and the ricotta has coloured on top, the pies should be ready. Remove from the oven and serve in those dishes if they look presentable.

Wood-fired Brick Oven with Enclosed Dome

You can learn a lot about oven making from books, but the practical experience (and trials and errors) of Andrew and Keith will help you avoid some of the traps for younger players.

by Andrew and Keith Cowley

MANSON LAKES, SOUTH AUSTRALIA

I HAVE always liked cooking over an open fire so building a brick oven was a natural extension of this. I have been using mine since 2005 and it's the heart of my suburban back yard. When my new house was finished I had two pallets of bricks and a pile of brickies' sand left over destined for landfill, so I figured I could use them and build something later. I came across Russell Jeavons book *Your Brick Oven: Building It and Baking In It* and visited his restaurant to see his two ovens and it went from there. Now the book doesn't tell you everything so I will detail a few of the lessons I learned.

First I dug the raft slab footing 1500 mm x 1500 mm with the perimeter 200 mm trenched to 400 mm deep to support the brick walls and to save on cement. I removed about eight (heaped) wheelbarrow loads of dirt and put in 50 mm of compacted crushed rock. Then I lined it with plastic, reinforcing rod and mesh. I used a cubic metre of sand/metal and two 40 kg bags of cement for the concrete slab. Once the slab went off I put the damp course down and started laying the bricks. I made about nine wheelbarrow loads of mortar using one 40 kg bag of Brighton lite cement, one 40 kg bag of hydrated lime (don't get it on bare legs — it burns!) and brickies' sand mixed at one part cement, one part lime and six parts brickies' sand.

This was enough for the nine courses of bricks to make the base for the dome and the recess at the front for the ash box. Once the bricks had gone off I filled the cavity of the base with 21 wheelbarrow loads of dry

Use dry sand to form the dome to prevent it sticking to the mortar.

site soil and compacted it as I went.

I then added two courses of compacted brickies' sand and placed two layers of clay pavers (stretcher bond pattern approximately 60 pavers per course) on top to bring it up to the finished level and form the level sole or floor of the oven. Then I spread over paving sand to fill in the gaps and an edge strip of wet cement to haunch the pavers and secure them in place. This also means that you can't replace the floor of the oven if you use this method.

Paying the price

The dome had to be 1000 mm inside diameter and set back 270 mm at the front to allow for the smoke chamber. The book suggests 1100 mm inside diameter, but that won't fit — it doesn't allow for the thickness of the dome bricks and the outside wall. I managed to buy 120 pressed red bricks (salvage yard) that were cut in half for the dome. This is a noisy and dusty job with a cutting disc! I then placed a circle on the floor of the oven made of black plastic to protect it and define the inside edge of the oven.

My father did all the metal work for the oven and made the steel arch for the opening 540 mm wide, 300 mm high and 6 mm thick. We used the dome gauge idea out of the book and started laying the dome, cut side of the half bricks facing out. We made sure the inside corners of the bricks touched, like a wedge, so more mortar was on the outside of the oven.

The first course was laid on a bed of mortar on top of the pavers using 25 half bricks (hb). The second course was 25 hb, the third course 22, fourth course 20, fifth course 19, and the sixth course was 20 hb. This was over the top of the arch. A sand mould as described in the book was built inside the oven. To support the next four courses of bricks (about 40 hb in total) until the mortar dried, I used moist sand for the mould and paid the price, as it stuck to the mortar inside the oven. So once the oven was finished I had to lie on my back and climb in the oven and scrub it off with a wire brush!

Once the dome had dried I rendered the outside with mortar to tie it together and removed the sand

The oven looking good on its first firing.

mould. This is exciting once you clean out the inside and can see the floor and all the half bricks in neat circular rows. Then the smoke chamber with its 150 mm diameter flue flange was fitted to the front of the oven and three sections of 150 mm diameter stainless steel flue (at $30 per section) were attached. Refer to the diagram on this page for dimensions of the smoke chamber as this wasn't in the book. At this stage you can use the oven but I decided to follow the book and extend the wall up another five courses and enclose the dome. The void was then filled with perlite to provide insulation (which means less firewood and it retains heat longer). To cap the top of the oven I used aluminium foil on top of the perlite and chicken wire then mortared it in a dome shape (to let rain run off).

Final tip

Go and buy an oven thermometer and when you do the first firing take care you don't lose your eyelashes when cooking — it gets hot!

Reference

Jeavons, Russell (2004). *Your Brick Oven: Building It and Baking In It.* Wakefield Press. ISBN 1 86254 661 4.

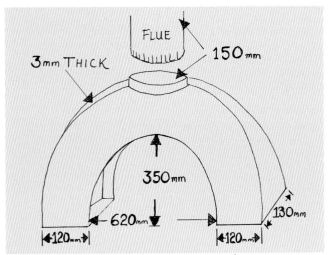

Smoke chamber detail, (not to scale).

Salt Dough Oven-baked Chicken with Roast Vegetables

In this recipe, once the whole chicken has been seasoned, stuffed and tied, it's browned then wrapped in oiled baking paper and covered with a salt dough to seal in all the cooking juices and cooked in the wood oven. The benefit of this dish is that once it's in the oven you don't have to touch it while it's cooking.

Ingredients

1 chicken (2 kg for 4 people)

Salt and pepper

Olive oil

Rind of 3 lemons

2–3 cloves of garlic crushed

1/2 bunch rosemary

1/2 bunch thyme

1/2 bunch oregano

Stuffing ingredients (your choice)

Butcher's twine for trussing the chicken

Vegetables

Pumpkin sliced

Shallots whole

Potatoes halved

Sweet potato (chop same size as potatoes)

Salt dough

1 kg cooking salt

1 kg plain flour

500–600 ml water

Make the salt dough in a large bowl by combining the salt and flour — make a well in the middle and add most of the water. Start to form the dough by kneading with hands — this is good exercise! You are done once you have a firm but malleable dough. Place in a lightly greased bowl and cover with plastic wrap and rest it for an hour. With the dough at room temperature roll it out onto a well floured bench about 5 mm thick. If you do it in two sheets it's easier so you end up with the bottom and top sheet of dough.

Wipe out the inside of the cavity of the chicken with paper towel to remove any traces of the innards and rinse with cold water. Coat the outsides of the chicken with olive oil, lemon rind, sea salt, pepper, crushed garlic, rosemary, thyme and oregano. Stuff the chicken with your favourite stuffing mix (as long as it's moist). I use a handful of mixed herb sprigs, a couple of shallots and two cloves of garlic. Using twine, truss the chicken at the front and rear if you wish, but it's not essential. I then brown the chicken top and bottom in an oven tray in the brick oven. You don't have to but if you don't the chicken once cooked and removed from the dough can look a bit pale.

Once the chicken has been browned remove from the oven. Cover in olive oil so the baking paper won't stick then wrap up the chicken. Put the bottom sheet of dough on a pizza peel* that has been sprinkled with flour. Place the wrapped chicken on top of the bottom sheet of dough. Put the second sheet of dough on top of the chicken and press the two sheets together (like a big pastie) making sure there are no holes. If you roll the bottom sheet up the side a bit this will help keep the cooking juices from running out. Push the fire to the back of the oven using a hoe to make space for the chicken and the baking tray for the vegetables. Slide the chicken parcel into the oven using the peel straight onto the floor.

Bake the chicken for 30 minutes at 220°C and then for 90 minutes at 160°C. Once the chicken has been in for 30 minutes put in the vegetables in a baking tray alongside it until cooked, making sure they are well oiled and seasoned. You will need to flip the vegetables half way through the cooking process so they cook on both sides.

Once roast vegetables are cooked (check with a skewer) then remove the baked chicken parcel from the oven. Gently crack the top of the dough open with the back of a large knife and peel off the baking paper (you will start to smell it now) and serve in the bottom sheet of dough which will be full of hot flavoured cooking juice. Don't eat the cooked dough — it's too salty! Enjoy with the roast vegetables!

*Pizza peel is the name for the flat stainless steel paddle with a wooden handle used to slide pizza in and out of the oven.

Rocks and Bricks

Using recycled materials and ingenuity, Sally created a rustic but effective oven featuring canine cooking timers.

by Sally McDonald
HEALESVILLE, VICTORIA

Under construction: the roof of Sally's oven is a washing machine drum on its side, to which she welded a fame to hold a door from a salvaged combustion stove.

I'VE BEEN an avid reader of alternative lifestyle magazines for several years and, like many, long to escape suburbia for a quieter life in the country. I've tried to make my quarter acre as rustic and relaxing as possible, somewhere to unwind, and to that end was inspired by the many backyard ovens in the mags to build my own.

First I laid a concrete base, and more by luck than design, really, began piling up rocks, bricks and bits of concrete into a shape I hoped would stand up to at least a few pizzas before it fell over. The fire is built on an old barbie grate, over which I set a solid cast alloy plate. Sitting on top of that is a washing machine drum on its side, to which I welded a frame to hold an old door from a combustion stove, salvaged from the local tip.

I kept piling up rocks and bricks until I reached the desired height and shape, incorporating a piece of terracotta drainpipe, which in turn, holds the flue.

When all was set I gave it a test run, and apart from a few cracks in the mortar, it went like a dream. I've used it to make pizzas, curries, roast chicken, lamb and pork, and a lovely rainbow trout, all to mouthwatering perfection. I always know when the food's ready: my two little dogs, Jess and Penny, sit hopefully in front of the oven, sniffing the delicious aromas and waiting to be my taste testers.

RECIPES

Pizza

Make a dough from 2 cups SR flour, a pinch of salt, 1/2 cup milk, 1/2 cup vegie oil, and roll or punch out on a tray.

Spread with 1/2 tomato paste and 1/2 barbecue sauce, mixed.

Sprinkle with tasty cheese and top with mushrooms, capsicum, onion, bacon, tomato, and anything else you fancy, then top with shredded mozzarella.

Cook until the smell tells you it's ready.

Roast Lamb with Rosemary & Garlic

Take a leg of lamb, wash, and poke holes in it with a sharp knife. Separate a bulb of garlic and chop some sprigs of rosemary. Push a clove of garlic and a sprig of rosemary into each hole. Sprinkle with seasoning or salt and place in a deep tray. Pour in about an inch of water and cover with aluminium foil.

Roast for about 1 1/2 hours, or until juice runs clear. If you like the outside crisp, take the foil off for the last half hour.

Baked Trout

Take your fish. I use rainbow trout, but I suppose anything could be used.

Clean it and wash thoroughly, lay on aluminium foil and sprinkle with chopped herbs, a few dobs of butter and a big squeeze of lemon. Add salt if desired. Wrap in foil and cook for about 3/4 of an hour, check at about 1/2 an hour — you don't want it to dry out.

Enjoy!!

Bread Dough: The Right Stuff

As Brendan explains, you can't make a good loaf unless you get the dough right. Let him take you through it step-by-step.

by Brendan Carter

BALLARAT, VICTORIA

IN RECENT times homemade bread has become very popular again. Instead of being a necessity people are making it for self-satisfaction and because they can't purchase the style of bread they require, generally with good flavour.

It will come down to personal preference, but the biggest problem most people have with their breads is that they don't mix the dough enough. In my years of baking I can guarantee that you won't over mix a dough by hand; the opposite is most common — under mixing. Even using breadmaking machines, I question how a small 20 to 30 mm agitator can mix a dough of approximately 1 kg flour weight.

Wheaten flour for bread making contains two gluten-forming proteins: glutenin, which gives extensibility, and gliadin, which gives elasticity. These proteins, when hydrated and mixed, form a glutinous network which encapsulates the gases produced from the yeast (natural or commercial), in turn allowing the dough to rise. If you don't develop (mix) these proteins enough you will end up with a heavy, dense structure to your bread. This bread will also have poor keeping qualities.

Is the dough mixed enough?

The simplest way to determine if your dough is mixed is to do the 'window test'. This involves taking a small piece of dough, making it into a ball and slowly stretching it out to see how thin you can get it. If the dough breaks easily, mix it more. You should be able to stretch out the trial piece to form a thin, even piece of dough. You should almost be able to read the newspaper through it. When this is achieved your dough is mixed.

Basic Bread Formula

Flour 0.500 units, Salt 0.010, Caster sugar 0.005
Olive oil 0.010   Dry yeast 0.007 (1 sachet)
Or Compressed yeast 0.020 (1/3 of the strength of dry yeast)
Water (tepid) 0.300 +/-

If using compressed yeast make sure it does not come in contact with the salt or sugar as this will have a retarding effect on the performance of the yeast.

Water is always variable. If the dough feels wet, dust with a little flour. If dough feels stiff, add a little water.

The dough should have a feel that is nice and soft with a slight stickiness to it.

Method

1. Mix all dry ingredients together. Form a well in the centre.
2. Pour water and oil into centre of well. Working the flour

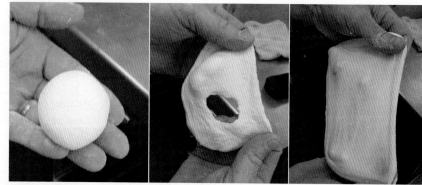

To test if your dough is mixed enough, take a small piece ... and stretch it. If it tears, go back to work ... until you can almost read through it.

from the inside bottom of the well, mix with liquid and make a slurry in the centre.

3. Slowly work all flour mix into slurry and mix together. A good action to do this is to stretch the dough out and roll it back towards yourself, then stretch again and so on, making sure you work all areas of the dough.

4. Continue mixing until you think it is mixed, and then give it a bit more. If you put a fair amount of energy into the dough, mixing should take approximately 10 to 15 minutes. If you do it a little slower you will need to mix longer. Think of it as an upper body workout!

5. When dough is mixed, round up into a smooth round ball and allow to rest for 10 to 15 minutes (the dough, not you: you should be cleaning up the mess you make in the kitchen), making sure you cover the dough with a cloth to protect it from the elements.

6. This dough will be enough to make one large loaf or two small loaves. If you want it can be broken into smaller pieces for bread rolls as well.

7. After the first rest, divide your dough into required sizes and round up again, allowing another 10 to 15 minutes rest, again keeping dough covered.

8. Mould the dough pieces into required shapes. When moulding it is best to degas the loaf first then shape. It is important to degas the dough as this process helps breakdown starch particles in the flour, which are then converted into fermentable sugars for the yeast to feed off.

9. Cover the dough pieces for final proof. A damp tea towel can be used which will keep the dough surface moist, allowing it to rise without forming a skin or splitting. Sit dough in a warm position and allow to rise.

10. Bake bread in a warm oven (210°C) for approximately 20 minutes for small units, and approximately 45 minutes for large loaves.

11. When you think bread is baked, pick it up and tap the base of the loaf. If it sounds hollow, it should be baked.

All ovens (convection, fan-forced, wood-fired) are different, therefore it can be trial and error until you get the perfect loaf. Keep trying and good luck.

Chapter Three

If You Can't Build Your Own...

Vesuvio Woodfired Ovens

Vesuvio ovens, originating from the Tuscany region of Italy, come in several models and sizes.

by Joe Cassisi
REVESBY, NEW SOUTH WALES

VESUVIO ovens are manufactured using refractory materials. The cooking floor, of cotto clay quarried from the hills of Tuscany, is perfectly smoothed, eliminating foreign smells and tastes, and aids perfect cooking of pizzas, baked dishes and other foods.

The ovens can be installed indoors or outdoors and can run on wood alone, gas/wood combination or gas alone. They are versatile in use, being suitable for baking, braising, stewing, sautéing, frilling, smoking, roasting and searing in juices. The oven maintains moisture and flavour and prevents food from drying. A pizza will cook to perfection in only three minutes.

• *For further information contact Vesuvio on (02) 9792 4999 or visit their website www.woodfiredovens.net.*

The cooking floor, of cotto clay quarried from the hills of Tuscany, is perfectly smoothed. Haberfield, Sydney.

Vesuvio ovens can be installed indoors or outdoors and can run on wood alone, gas/wood combination or gas alone. Elizabeth Bay, Sydney.

Smoked Salmon Pizza

Ingredients
2 x dough balls (see pizza dough recipe)
2/3 cup pizza sauce (pureed peeled tomatoes seasoned with salt, basil and oregano)
1 1/2 cups grated mozzarella
1 Spanish red onion, sliced thinly
1 tablespoon small capers, rinsed of salt or brine
1/4 bunch chives, chopped
200 g sliced smoked salmon
freshly cracked pepper
100 g sour cream
Makes 2 medium pizzas

Method
Roll out your pizza bases. Cover the bases with the pizza sauce. Sprinkle the mozzarella over the base, keeping 2 cm away from the edge of the dough.

Place the sliced onion on the base. Scoop the pizzas onto a paddle and slide into the oven. Bake pizzas for 2 to 3 minutes. Whilst pizzas are baking, gently turn the pizzas in a circular direction allowing it to brown the edges all over.

Remove the pizzas from the wood-fired oven, place slices of smoked salmon on the base, sprinkle capers and garnish with chives. Season with freshly cracked black pepper. Place a dollop of sour cream in the middle, cut into slices and serve immediately.

Alfresco Wood Fired Pizza Ovens

These ovens offer considerable freedom for individual customising, and may be fixed in place or movable.

The Alfresco range comes in two sizes, and can be supplied ready to go.

by Jonelle Lowe
CHIDLOW, WESTERN AUSTRALIA

ALFRESCO Wood Fired Pizza Ovens are an economical and efficient alternative to the traditional Aussie barbecue. They require less maintenance than a barbecue and no cleaning. Available in a range of colours and finishes, the ovens can be custom designed to best suit your entertainment area.

And when cooking in your Alfresco oven, don't just think pizzas — think about roasting, slow cooking, smoking, drying fruits, baking breads and grilling.

The Original Alfresco oven is the largest oven and is supplied as a finished unit. The Alfresco offers an expansive internal cooking area, allowing a whole sheep or goat or up to six 30 cm diameter pizzas to be cooked at once.

The Courtyard model is Alfresco's smaller unit, designed to fit into smaller courtyards and entertaining areas. It will fit two 30 cm pizzas or two roasting trays at a time. The Courtyard model is also available in either a basic or full DIY kit.

Prices start from $900. Alfresco also make a variety of steel stands on which to sit your oven for those who want a more portable option.

And for a really portable option, why not try Alfresco's trailer-mounted oven? It is available for hire and provides a practical solution to catering for parties and other functions.

• For more information contact Geoff Chilman on 0417 988 614 or visit their website: www. alfresco woodfiredovens.com.au

Basic Pizza Dough
Ingredients
- *3 kg bakers' flour*
- *1 tbsp dried yeast*
- *1 tbsp salt*
- *1 tbsp sugar*
- *1 tbsp baking powder*
- *1.25 L – 1.5 L water*
- *50 ml extra virgin olive oil*

Method
1. Combine flour with salt, sugar and water. Mix until well formed dough is attained.
2. In a separate bowl add a small amount of tepid water to yeast and stir until dissolved.
3. Add the yeast, baking powder and olive oil to the dough and knead until combined.
4. Refrigerate for at least 24 hours before using.
Makes 15 to 20 pizzas.

Basic Pizza Sauce
Ingredients
- *1 x 400 g can chopped tomatoes*
- *Handful of fresh basil, chopped*
- *30 ml extra virgin olive oil*
- *Fresh garlic according to taste, crushed*
- *Pinch of salt*

Method
Combine all ingredients in blender and spread evenly over prepared pizza base.

Try blending sun-dried tomatoes in olive oil with basil, garlic and seasonings for a richer flavour.

Al Forno Wood Fired Ovens

Traditionally, Italian ovens were made with bricks and took time and expertise to build. But Al Forno ovens, imported directly from Italy, come in kit form and are easy to install.

by Maurelio Gabrielli and Robert Cusenza

TOORAK GARDENS, SOUTH AUSTRALIA

AT 89 years of age, Giuseppina Cusenza still makes bread in her wood-fired oven. It has been a family tradition that she's passed on to her seven children, who all now have their own wood-fired ovens.

Of Italian upbringing, Maurelio Gabrielli and Robert Cusenza, the founders of Al Forno Wood Fired Ovens, have for three years now been supplying and installing these ovens all over the country.

Making your own wood oven bread and pizzas is a lot easier than you may think, and in 30 minutes the Al Forno oven is hot enough to begin cooking. But bread and pizza aside, you can cook almost anything in a wood-fired oven, from meat roasts and vegies to oysters Kilpatrick.

The Al Forno wood-fired oven is a quick and easy way to cook gourmet food in your own home.

• *For more information visit the Al Forno website: www. alforno.com.au.*

Giuseppina Cusenza prepares a batch of dough.

A baker's peel dusted with cornmeal is used to slip the pizza dough onto the grill and turn it over.

RECIPES

Italian Pizza Dough

2 cups warm water

2 pkt yeast

1 tsp salt

3 tbsp salad oil

4 cups flour

Dissolve yeast in warm water in bowl.

After dissolving, add salt, oil and flour. Mix well.

Turn on floured board and knead, add flour as needed.

Place in oiled bowl, and let rise, about 2 hours in warm place.

Pizza Bianca

A pizza without tomato sauce, this recipe is delicious, topped only with prosciutto and peppery Arugula. Makes 4 individual pizzas.

4 individual pizza dough balls, defrosted

2 cups fresh washed Arugula

Prosciutto

1 oz shaved parmesan cheese

Olive oil for drizzling

Cook the pizza dough completely, then top with first the prosciutto, then the Arugula, and finally the cheese. Drizzle a little olive oil over each pizza and serve. We like to use hot oil that we have made by soaking red pepper flakes in a good quality olive oil for a week or more. It adds just an extra bite to the pizza! Buon appetito!

DIY Pizza Ovens

by Mark Fay

FREMANTLE, WESTERN AUSTRALIA

E VER wanted to build you own DIY pizza oven? Well now you can. It's a fun, easy and affordable design for anyone to assemble with no previous experience necessary. The kits use the latest technology of advanced high temperature refractory bricks assembled in the traditional way. The oven can be decorated however you like to match your home or garden. The pizza oven cooks food quickly, and the intense heat seals in the flavour and juices of the food. All the components of your DIY oven are supplied.

The ovens come in three sizes, ranging in price from $990 to $1390. Every Wednesday night in Fremantle we hold free DIY pizza oven demonstrations (bookings are essential).

The DIY pizza oven can be decorated any way you like.

• *Terracotta Tile Co. 5 James Street, Fremantle, WA, 6160. Ph: (08) 9336 1240 Fax: 9430 8285, www. diypizzaovens.com.au.*

Kate inspects the tile inlay: your own choice of materials can add much to the oven.

Suppliers and Further Reading

Oven Material Suppliers

You can contact these suppliers for firebricks, tiles, refractory, bags of castable, high temperature mortar, vermiculite, ceramic fire blanket, air setting cement, and stainless steel needles. Many of the suppliers below have been generously provided by Alan Watt.

Field Furnace Pty Ltd, 8 Arnott Place, Wetherill Park, phone (02) 9729 1799.

Refractory & Ceramics Pty Ltd, 50 Geddes St, Mulgrave, Victoria, phone (03) 9560 4477.

Darley Refractories, 50 Grey St, Bacchus March, Victoria, phone (03) 5367 2300.

Eureka Tiles, Ballarat, phone 1300 387 352 or Austral Brick agencies for Bowral brick pavers, 500 mm and 65 mm and Bowral pressed solid bricks.

Major plant nurseries and hydroponic suppliers sell vermiculite, and perlite for approximately $35 to $45.

Most landscape suppliers sell decomposed granite (granitic sand) and brickies' sand.

Barbeques Galore outlets sell stainless steel flue pipe (4 inch for approximately $30 per section), bales of rockwool, and brass barbecue cleaning brushes (for scraping the floor of your oven).

Costante Engineering, 377-379 Bell St, Preston, phone (03) 9484 7948, sell brass brush heads and temperature gauges.

Readybuilt Oven Kits

Alfresco Wood Fired Pizza Ovens. Phone (08) 9304 6337 or (08) 9572 3696. Web: www.alfrescowoodfiredovens.com.au

Vesuvio Woodfired Ovens. 40/65 Marigold Street, Revesby, NSW, 2212, phone (02) 9792 4999. Web: www. woodfiredovens.net

Al Forno Wood Ovens. Phone (08) 8364 1857 or (08) 8379 9494. Web: www.alforno.com.au

Terracotta Tile Company, 5 James Street, Fremantle, 6160. Phone (08) 9336 1240, web: www.diypizzaovens.com.au

Beech Ovens. 36 Gladys St, Stones Corner, Brisbane Qld, 4120, Australia. Phone (07) 3397 0277, website: www. beechovens.com.au

Pivot Stove. Phone 1300 432 837, 234 - 238 Moorabool Street, Geelong, Victoria 3220. Web: www.pivotstove.com.au

Ima Forni. Phone (03) 9460 6808, web: www.imaforni.com.au

Golden Ember. PO Box 8171, Carrum Down LPO, Victoria, 3201, phone (03) 5996 3203, web: www.in-flame.com.au.

Tutto Pizza. 176 Stirling Highway, Claremont, WA, 6010, phone (08) 9386 8933, web: www.tuttopizza.com.au.

Pizza Trays, Peels, cooking equipment etc

Temperature Controls (for oven temperature gauges), 7 Yamma St, Sefton, NSW, phone (02) 9721 8644.

PWS Hospitality Supplies, 58 Maryborough St, Fyshwick, ACT, phone (02) 6239 2189.

Euroquip. Unit 40, 65 Marigold Street, Revesby, NSW 2212, phone (02) 9792 4999, web: www.euroquip.com.au.

ABP Atlas, 122 Whitehorse Road, Blackburn, Victoria, 3130, phone (03) 9878 6900, web: www.abpatlas.com.au.

V-I-P Catering Equipment, 144 - 148 Plenty Road, Preston, Victoria, phone (03) 9480 3777, web: www.v-i-p.com.au.

Caterers Warehouse, Shop 4, 241 The Entrance Road, Erina, NSW, 2251, phone (02) 4365 1699, web: www. catererswarehouse.com.au.

Further Information

Ovencrafters. Alan Scott, web: www.ovencrafters.net.

Further Reading

The Bread Builders*, Alan Scott and Daniel Wing, Chelsea Green.

Your Brick Oven*, Russell Jeavons, Wakefield Press.

Build Your Own Earth Oven*, Kiko Denzer, Hand Print Press.

*These books available from www.goodlifebookclub.com, phone (03) 5424 1814.

Index

You've Bought The Book Now Try The Magazine

... Free

FREE sample of 'Earth Garden' magazine.
Fax or post a photocopy of this page: we'll post you one sample.
EARTH GARDEN IS AVAILABLE FROM NEWSAGENTS, OR HOME-DELIVERED BY SUBSCRIPTION. Four times a year we cover:

- Back yard ovens, DIY building projects, stone, brick, and earth building, plus healthy cuisine and renewable energy.
- Organic gardening and permaculture.
- Solar hot water, DIY projects, energy-saving tips.

Name . . . .

Address. . . . .

. . . . .P/code . . . .

Where did you buy Back Yard Ovens? . . . .
POST: Earth Garden, PO Box 2 Trentham, Vic, 3458 **OR FAX** to us at: (03) 5424 1743.
For more information, visit our website at www.earthgarden.com.au, and follow the 'Earth Garden Path' links to join our up-to-the-minute, natural building discussions and back yard DIY projects.

Three oven-building books from
The Good Life Book Club

Australia's no-obligation book club for simpler, healthier lifestyles.

The Bread Builders
Daniel Wing & Alan Scott
$65.00 inc GST
Even if you never build one of the elegant masonry brick bread ovens detailed in this hugely informative book, the wisdom about natural bread baking by Australian, Alan Scott, will leave you very satisfied. With this book you will want to bake naturally-fermented hearth loaves with the finest quality leavens and whole grains. Essential for any good lifer's library. 253 pages.

Build Your Own Earth Oven
Kiko Denzer,
$39.95 inc GST
These designs would fit perfectly in just about everyone's backyard. This book has fully illustrated, step-by-step directions on how to build a low-cost, wood-fired mud oven, how to tend the fire, and make perfect sourdough loaves. The materials will cost you from zero to $50. 132 pages.

Your Brick Oven
Russell Jeavons
$29.95 inc GST
An Australian guide to building the ultimate brick oven — and modern recipes that reflect multicultural tastes. The author — a successful brick oven restaurateur—shows with clear drawings and instructions how to build your own brick oven for those magical nights when you can cook up a storm and not be tied to your kitchen stove. Don't just cook (heavenly) pizza — what about Turkish pide, roasts, bread, fish or cakes? 84 pages.

Phone (03) 5424 1814, or visit:
www.goodlifebookclub.com
for secure ordering online.